Locales

Locales

Poems from the Fellowship of Southern Writers

Edited by FRED CHAPPELL
With a Foreword by GEORGE GARRETT

 Louisiana State University Press   *Baton Rouge*

Copyright © 2003 by Louisiana State University Press
Manufactured in the United States of America
First printing

12 11 10 09 08 07 06 05 04 03
5 4 3 2 1

Designer: Amanda McDonald Scallan
Typeface: Sabon
Typesetter: Coghill Composition Co. Inc.
Printer and binder: Thomson-Shore, Inc.

Library of Congress Cataloging-in-Publication Data:

Locales : poems from the Fellowship of Southern Writers / edited by Fred Chappell;
with a foreword by George Garrett.
        p.   cm.
    ISBN 0-8071-2863-5 (alk. paper)—ISBN 0-8071-2864-3 (pbk. : alk. paper)
    1. American poetry—Southern States.   2. Southern States—Poetry.   I. Chappell, Fred,
1936– II. Fellowship of Southern Writers.

PS551.L63   2003
811′.54080975—dc21   2002035920

The paper in this book meets the guidelines for permanence and durability of the Committee on
Production Guidelines for Book Longevity of the Council on Library Resources. ⊗

Contents

Foreword

The idea of the Fellowship of Southern Writers came from the late
Cleanth Brooks, who had been thinking of the need for some sort of or-
ganization aimed at encouraging Southern literature in general and, espe-
cially, offering some kind of formal recognition to young Southern
writers. In 1987 while Brooks was visiting Chapel Hill, he talked about
the idea at some length with scholar Louis D. Rubin, Jr., and together
they decided to begin. On September 18, 1987, Brooks sent out a letter
to a varied group of Southern writers, saying: "For some time several of
us have been discussing the need for, and the possibility of founding, a
society or fellowship of Southern writers." The writers were invited "to
meet and establish an organization to encourage and recognize distinc-
tion in Southern writing." The meeting was scheduled for and held on
October 30–31 in Chattanooga.

Why Chattanooga? First of all, because it already had a highly suc-
cessful Biennial Conference on Southern Literature, created by the Arts
and Education Council there, one which had built up the widespread
support of the local community. Louis D. Rubin, Jr., who, together with

George Core, editor of the *Sewanee Review,* joined Cleanth Brooks in arranging the first meeting, says that Chattanooga and its conference seemed especially appropriate because of "the fact that it was a civic and not an academic undertaking and equally that it was not identified with any one school or group or coterie or a particular kind of Southern writing." This latter goal, literary neutrality, was more important than one might have imagined: "The two universities most active in contemporary Southern letters, Vanderbilt University and the University of North Carolina at Chapel Hill, were good possibilities for a home. But each of them was associated with a particular group of writers, and we did not want the Fellowship to fall under the aegis—no matter how benevolent—of any one group." On June 22, Rubin, Brooks, and Core met with Chattanooga community leaders at the offices of the Lyndhurst Foundation, from whom the Fellowship received both an organizational grant and, later, a development grant. The organizational meeting of the Fellowship took place in October 1987. Those present included Cleanth Brooks, Fred Chappell, George Core, Shelby Foote, George Garrett, Blyden Jackson, Andrew Lytle, Lewis P. Simpson, Elizabeth Spencer, Walter Sullivan, C. Vann Woodward, and Louis D. Rubin, Jr. Not present at the meeting, but already committed to support of the Fellowship were Eudora Welty, Robert Penn Warren, Peter Taylor, Walker Percy, Ernest J. Gaines and John Hope Franklin. Says Rubin:

> We wanted to encourage and stimulate good writing in the South. While we didn't think of our group as competing with any of the national academies and institutes—to which many of our group already belonged—we wanted the work of young Southern authors to be read and evaluated and recognized by other Southern writers for whom the region and the subject matter would not seem 'quaint' or 'exotic.' But at the same time we wanted to recognize and encourage only work of the highest quality, free from insularity and localism. And we wanted our members to include not only novelists, poets, dramatists and critics, but writers of history and other genres whose work displayed literary excellence.

Cleanth Brooks was chosen to be the first chancellor of the Fellowship; Louis D. Rubin, Jr., was named chairman of the executive committee;

George Core was chosen to be secretary-treasurer; and George Garrett became vice chancellor. In addition to the eighteen writers already committed, James Dickey, Ralph Ellison, Reynolds Price, and William Styron joined the others and all were constituted as founding members of the Fellowship.

At the outset the Fellowship agreed to hold a meeting and an awards convocation in conjunction with the regular Biennial Conference on Southern Literature. The University of Tennessee at Chattanooga offered to house the archives of the Fellowship at the Lupton Library. The Fellowship set out to secure endowments from which prizes would be awarded to younger Southern writers. One form of recognition of distinction would be membership in the Fellowship. And the highest award, given for a lifetime's achievement in letters, would be a medal which the original membership, without consulting its first chancellor, named the Cleanth Brooks Medal.

Soon the Fellowship was incorporated under the law. It received a development grant from the Lyndhurst Foundation to cover operating expenses and such incidental costs as the casting of bronze medallions for the individual Fellows. Photographer Curt Richter was commissioned to photograph each Fellow, and the photographs are on display in the Fellowship's Archive Room, renamed in 1997 the Arlie Herron Room in honor of the professor of Southern literature at the University of Tennessee at Chattanooga. And in the months prior to the first full-scale meeting and convocation of the Fellowship, endowments for the various awards were secured. The Hillsdale Foundation created the Hillsdale Prize for Fiction. The James G. Hanes Foundation offered a Hanes Prize in Poetry. Chubb Life supported the Robert Penn Warren Award in fiction, and the Bryan Family Foundation financed an award in drama. The Fellows themselves contributed funds for an award in nonfiction and for the Fellowship's New Writing Award.

After two terms of two years as chancellor, Cleanth Brooks was followed, in turn, by Louis D. Rubin, Jr., George Garrett, Doris Betts, and Walter Sullivan. Ellen Douglas is now vice chancellor. The full membership of the Fellowship now included James Applewhite, Richard Bausch, Madison Smartt Bell, Wendell Berry, Doris Betts, Joseph Blotner, Fred

Chappell, George Core, Ellen Douglas, Clyde Edgerton, Horton Foote, Shelby Foote, John Hope Franklin, Ernest J. Gaines, George Garrett, Kaye Gibbons, Gail Godwin, Allan Gurganus, Barry Hannah, Beth Henley, William Hoffman, Josephine Humphreys, Blyden Jackson, Madison Jones, Donald Justice, Yusef Komunyakaa, Romulus Linney, Bobbie Ann Mason, Jill McCorkle, Marsha Norman, Reynolds Price, John Shelton Reed, Louis D. Rubin, Jr., Mary Lee Settle, Lewis P. Simpson, Dave Smith, Lee Smith, Elizabeth Spencer, William Styron, Walter Sullivan, Henry Taylor, Ellen Bryant Voight, Allen Wier, and Charles Wright.

In the years since its beginning, a number of Fellows have died: A. R. Ammons, Cleanth Brooks, James Dickey, Ralph Ellison, C. Eric Lincoln, Andrew Lytle, Walker Percy, Monroe K. Spears, Peter Taylor, Robert Penn Warren, and C. Vann Woodward.

Beginning with the first formal convocation of the Fellowship in 1989, awards have been presented to the following Southern writers: Hillsdale Prize for Fiction—Ellen Douglas (1989), Richard Bausch (1991), Josephine Humphreys (1993), William Hoffman (1995), Lewis Nordan (1997), Bobbie Ann Mason (1999), Perceval Everett (2001); Hanes Prize for Poetry—Kelly Cherry (1989), Robert Morgan (1991), Ellen Bryant Voigt (1993), Andrew Hudgins (1995), Yusef Komunyakaa (1997), T. R. Hummer (1999), Rodney Jones (2001); Chubb Award for Fiction in Honor of Robert Penn Warren—Lee Smith (1991), Cormac McCarthy (1993), Madison Smartt Bell (1995), Allen Wier (1997), Barry Hannah (1999), Mary Hood (2001); Bryan Family Foundation Award for Drama—Jim Grimsley (1991), Pearl Cleage (1995), Naomi Wallace (1997), Margaret Edson (1999), John Henry Redwood (2001); Fellowship Award for Nonfiction—Samuel F. Pickering, Jr. (1991), John Shelton Reed 1995), Bailey White (1997), James Kibler (1999), Hal Crowther (2001); Fellowship's New Writing Award—William Henry Lewis (1997), Michael Knight (1999), John McManus (2001); Special Achievement Award—Andrew Lytle (1995), James Still (1997); James Still Award—Charles Frazier (1999), George Scarbrough (2001); Cleanth Brooks Medal for Distinguished Achievement in Southern Letters—John Hope Franklin (1989), Eudora Welty (1991), C. Vann Woodward

(1993), Lewis P. Simpson (1995), Louis D. Rubin, Jr. (1997), Shelby Foote (1999), and Elizabeth Spencer (2001).

In addition to their biennial meeting and the public awards convocation, the Fellows are active participants in the Chattanooga Conference on Southern Literature. They join in panel discussions, readings, and lectures, and the keynote address for the conference is given by a member of the Fellowship. In 1997 the speaker was novelist Ernest J. Gaines. Prizewinners visit local and area high schools and meet with students there.

The Fellowship has now been in existence and active for more than ten years. "We are beginning our second decade in excellent shape," Louis D. Rubin, Jr., says. "We are now firmly linked to the Chattanooga Conference and we have high hopes that we can play an ever more active part in recognizing and honoring achievement and encouraging excellence in Southern letters."

This anthology is made up of poetry by members of the Fellowship of Southern Writers and winners of the Hanes Prize for Poetry, selected and edited by Fred Chappell. It will be followed in due course by a gathering of nonfiction edited by George Core. Members and prizewinners have agreed that any and all earnings from this book will go to the Fellowship as a contribution to its modest endowment. It is our hope that all of these books will give to the reader a sense of the direction and development of southern writing in our time.

—*George Garrett*

Preface

This volume of poetry by members of the Fellowship of Southern Writers is a complement to, and in many respects a companion of, *The Cry of an Occasion,* a volume of fiction by the members. The latter volume was edited by Richard Bausch and published by Louisiana State University Press in 2001.

In his preface to that volume Mr. Bausch spoke of his happiness in being associated with the Fellowship, and I am pleased to avow a similar pleasure in editing this book. The poetry of the contemporary South does not perhaps attain to the fame of its fiction, but it is no less vital as a body of work and is as inventive and important.

It may be that the label "regional" is more harmful to the reputation of poetry than to that of fiction. Poetry is supposed, by its very nature, to strive for universal application, to approach ideals limited in no way by questions of setting or ostensible subject matter.

Yet speech that addresses universal concerns must take place some-where within the universe, and when that place is specific, the poetry has a greater force than a placeless poetry might have. William Blake, William Wordsworth, and W. B. Yeats understood that the general is most securely held to when in the grip of the particular, and our contemporary southern poets take this doctrine to heart.

I have tried to emphasize this truth with my choices of poems for *Locales*. Almost all the poems here are not just specific, not only regional, but tightly joined to highly particular places within the southern region. Place names abound in these pages, and each name contains or connotes a unique flavor of its own. Though the places are often small, the poems are not shallow in depth of feeling nor narrow in breadth of implication. The lens of particular place is capable of intense focus and of correspondingly strong force. Here, then, is a southern gazette of heart and mind with mountains and valleys, forests and farms, rivers and marshes, graveyards and barrooms—places that have resonated with the poetry these poets overheard and captured and imagined. Every site has its tone; southern locales sing with a choir of them.

—*Fred Chappell*

Locales

A. R. Ammons

I WENT BACK

I went back
to my old home
and the furrow
of each year
plowed like
surf across
the place had
not washed
memory away.

THIS BLACK RICH COUNTRY

Dispossess me of belief:
between life and me obtrude
no symbolic forms:

grant me no mission: let my
mystical talents be beasts
in dark trees: thin the wire

I limp in space, melt it
with quick heat, let me walk
or fall alone: fail

me in all comforts:
hide renown behind the tomb:
withdraw beyond all reach of faith:

leave me this black rich country,
uncertainty, labor, fear: do not
steal the rewards of my mortality.

ENFIELD FALLS

I don't understand why the stream
before the falls over by Enfield
reminds me of my own going through

things when it narrows to
a pass and sinks moiling through
a foot-wide sluice where the water's

so fast the banks back up: that
coming to a necessity, like being
born or dying or getting to the

dentist, that tensing up and speeding
up, turbulence, and then the
opening out on the other side, easing

up, turning into sheets mist-thin
falling, air's weight, over
the fall's edge: I don't know

why this is and is not like things
I've felt: they say nature is almost
contemptuously beneath me now, I'm so

separate, my destiny so different
from water's, and I agree, at least, in
part, but also I don't understand why

what I have to take on, tense to, seems
easier, clearer, and more to be expected
just because water expresses motions

that look like my emotions: if
we could be a little at home here! . . .
racing, falling, easing away.

GRAVELLY RUN

I don't know somehow it seems sufficient
to see and hear whatever coming and going is,
losing the self to the victory
    of stones and trees,
of bending sandpit lakes, crescent
round groves of dwarf pine:

for it is not so much to know the self
as to know it as it is known
    by galaxy and cedar cone,
as if birth had never found it
and death could never end it:

the swamp's slow water comes
down Gravelly Run fanning the long
    stone-held algal
hair and narrowing roils between
the shoulders of the highway bridge:

holly grows on the banks in the woods there,
and the cedars' gothic-clustered
    spires could make
green religion in winter bones:

so I look and reflect, but the air's glass
jail seals each thing in its entity:
no use to make any philosophies here:
    I see no
god in the holly, hear no song from
the snowbroken weeds: Hegel is not the winter
yellow in the pines: the sunlight has never
heard of trees: surrendered self among
    unwelcoming forms: stranger,
hoist your burdens, get on down the road.

ALLIGATOR HOLES DOWN ALONG
ABOUT OLD DOCK

Lord, I wish I were in Hallsboro, over by the tracks,
or somewhere down past the Green Swamp around Nakina, or
traipsing, dabbling in the slipping laps of Lake Waccamaw:

how I wish I were over by Fair
Bluff where the old Lumber River snakes under overhanging
cypress-moss, black glass going

gleamy deep and slow, 'gator easy and slow:
I bet a mockingbird's cutting loose a Dido in wisteria
vine or mimosa bush over there right now: if I were

down by Shalotte, the fish fries, scrubby sand-woods,
the beach dunes nearby: or Gause's Landing:
Lord, I wish I were home—those pastures—where I'll

never be again: Spring Branch Church, South
Whiteville, New Brunswick: mother and father, aunts,
uncles gone over, no one coming back again.

MOUNTAIN TALK

I was going along a dusty highroad
when the mountain
across the way
turned me to its silence:
oh I said how come
I don't know your
massive symmetry and rest:
nevertheless, said the mountain,
would you want
to be
lodged here with
a changeless prospect, risen
to an unalterable view:
so I went on
counting my numberless fingers.

James Applewhite

ROAD DOWN HOME

Out of range of the classical station, I enter
Country music bawling from Tarboro:
Cheating and endless loves, whiskey, whiskery lips—
So Joe Speight splitting down 264
In his boat of a Chrysler might be
My father in his outboard, plowing the new flood,
The beginning waters—when Red Hill was solitary Ararat.
Still it is similar. Radio's wails like wild dogs baying
Along bends of that old river back to Nineveh. Silver air.
Log barns with pediments tilting seem
Tumuli projecting from an ancienter landscape.
The mirroring I remember about his boat
Lies ponded from recent rain: openings
Into a moonlighted Atlantis
Where the barbed wire's stringers,
Over their heads in currents of the wild dogs' cry,
Left these lines of iron
Now passing through the hearts of timber trees.
In a ditch, the circle of a clearing.
Blue silhouetted with a cabin.
Owl's whoop staring. Stone moon.

A MAP OF SIMPLICITIES

The sawmill's whistle for noon would surprise us,
When it sounded so loud and close by. Afterward,

The noises felt farther away, and we thought
About living in the country by ourselves.
Our map to the camp looked serious and older.
The creek lined a border at the bottom,
Dark limbs marking the thickets. Then fields
With regular, combed-looking furrows held
New corn sparkling like broken green bottles
In rows in the sun. Backyards fenced off
From the plowed-up dirt kept chickens and gardens,
Then the town's white houses followed streets,
And railroad tracks were ridged like a backbone.
The side toward the creek went down into night,
But coming toward the stoplight seemed up into sun.
Our station burned bulbs above its columns,
And the sawmill cut lumber out of trees,
So carpenters could nail up new houses, and people
Move in, and look through the upstairs windows
Into air from the lonesome edge of town—
The map in my mind now brighter in consciousness.

SOUTHLAND DRIVE-IN

This is the obligatory Southern poem.
Will copperheads horny with venom twine
Cornerstones of mansions left charred by Sherman?
Listen, the field is paved, the only crop
Raised these speakers on poles. They crackle
With rumor, to boys with hand on the stick-shift,
Of the virgin who died impaled, after
Coca-Cola laced with Spanish Fly.
Fried chicken is eaten, not all the meat
Here is white, but even as a thunderhead
Slashes and cannonades, rendering heat
Into current, this living theater of bodies
Plays out its music—like a radio tuned
To a station from so far away, maybe
Latin America, its reception sounds eerie

With static and distance. Antennas catch
Signals from ditches, where frogs no bigger
Than the gonad-shaped pecans of the grove
Blow their bellies up to broadcast: *no matter,*
They say from the water, *we all here is*
Dark meat. Blacks run away to the swamps,
Slick with the rapes you wish your sisters.
The root of this plot, upraised on the screen,
Is poor white meat. And a wind comes
Sighing from the crowd, the great thundercrowd
In the mind of this Southern land. Some rain
Has fallen, little rivers trickled on the banks
Of back seats. Moccasins slide a soft water.

A WILSON COUNTY FARMER

The mercury-vapor yard light on a pole
    comes on automatically at dusk, triggered
it seems by the television's phosphorescent glow in
    the front room, seen incongruously through those
sashes and panes from just after the Civil War.
    The middle-aged farmer standing in shadow of this
unnatural light before his packhouse, still smoking
    a Lucky, just a few in any day now, sees
heads of his wife and daughter-in-law through the
    window, and the grandson's occasional, ball-quick
passage through color, and thinks maybe he has survived
    too long. Life is easier, maybe, with MH-30
to inhibit suckers, the tractor-drawn harvesters,
    where croppers ride close to the ground, breaking
off leaves, clipping them into the reeled chains. But hands
    are undependable, and without his blood kin,
a man couldn't hardly be sure of a harvest crew.
    Some use the migrants, hard-working, ignorant
of the ways of tobacco. With the quotas, the declining

prices, every day more news about cancer, this man
who learned tobacco from his father, who himself couldn't
    read and write, looks far across at red Antares
over the swamp woods there beyond the highway, not knowing
    what star he is seeing, and feels his station in this
place lit by blue light and T.V. as odd and as lonely.

THE VILLAGE AFTER SUNSET

The Town of Stantonsburg grew up at the intersection
of the Waynesboro-Tarboro road and Contentnea
Creek. Where these two arteries of transportation
met, the Stanton family built a landing. From this
landing naval stores, cotton and other produce were
shipped downstream to New Bern. Fertilizer and
other supplies from down stream were landed here.
    —*A History of Stantonsburg: Circa 1780–1980*

He remembers the village after sunset as in
    a space of gold leaf. Once nativities with
angels lay as flat against a sky thinned
    by time as this Protestant congregation,
rinsed by their hardship, waiting on new shore
    for revelation in a star. Their honest faces
had overseen the storefronts and steeple,
    houses determined in the squares and peaks
by need to keep heat and shed rain. Now
    light seeping back into space raised the town
into a flat elevation, like the set for a Western.
    That absolute contemplation, that tabula rasa
of light, stunned his mind. Simplicities
    occupied vision like fruit in a still life.
Revelation came not out of all-radiant
    space but from caves in the body. Animals
in their stables witnessed births of animals.
    Passageways showed where road or river

had framed a perspective. Only along these
    did change unfold, in a skin like a snake's:
an oily hieroglyphic writing a slither of
    becoming into scenes as if embroidery—
the house, the pickets, an oak with the leaves
    in cloud-shapes, as sun arced over in its
varying constancy. The well rope went
    down into a circular gaze, but this other
look brought the steamboat, in a simple
    apparition, out of bends of pure reflection.
The sun so flooded the senses in its synchronic
    origin, his eye had not imagined far sources.
The fierce blade of harvest and carpentry
    cut the serpent as it twined into innermost
recesses. Desire had unfolded without wisdom,
    following cascades in their musical cadences
when the spring flood had let Contentnea
    spread near the bridge, like an expansion
of vision. Then the packet came up as far
    as Stanton, bringing laces and fabrics.
An organ had rested perilously on the deck
    during the whole trip upriver from New Bern.
Christmas that year heard voices more nearly
    those of angels: children in the nativity
wearing aureoles of tinsel, as gold-leaf sunset
    framed the town in its permanent being.

WATER FROM THE LAMP BOTTLE

A few months later SEVEN SPRINGS HOTEL was opened.
Soon it was the mecca for society in Eastern Carolina.
Fine carriages, plumed hats, tight breeches and bat-wing
ties lent the resort a grace which is lacking today.
    —*Some Facts about Seven Springs Waters*, 1940

The grandfather's ten-gallon demijohn
    is stoppered with a lamp, a shade

disguising the mouth that blabbed out
    Seven Springs water. The sources of those
seven trickles—each supposedly with
    its own curative properties—were boxed
already by concrete, enclosed within octagonal
    latticework: wet tunnels in a wall, origin
of the sheen that overspread the floor slab
    like polish on marble. The Neuse drifted
darkly, smooth, enigmatic, seen by a child
    refreshed after drinking from the dipper,
feet tingling from the cold, surprised by a frog
    in the springhouse. Those beginnings that
brightened concrete, to be taken home in your own
    formulation in the oversized bottle, seemed
to him the source of the river. It slid there,
    slick against the underside of so much air—
air possessing, in the distance of its width,
    a blue tint of accumulated haze; air wet
with vapor, temperature eighties or nineties, clouds
    casting down white impressions of their bulks,
flattened there, stylized in two dimensions.
    So the scene itself seemed dual: a tintype
photograph versus the vivid present a child
    feels, scampering from a frog, desiring
Spanish moss as it waved in grandfatherly
    beards, spears on that swarthy surface: a corded,
sweat-oiled portrait of a life past representing.
    Fists and forearms of black men had worked
in strokes like pistons so that the steam barge
    could huff its vapor. The somnolent reflections
of bends fixed willows and the darting dragonfly.

HOME TEAM

There was a stillness about the games, afternoons,
    something to be decided, but in suspension—a runner

taking his lead as the pitcher eyed him suspiciously,
    the outfielders glancing back at the bushes thirty
feet to their rear, edging in a little, trying to remember
    the soft spots, where a line drive wouldn't bounce up.
Thunderheads building in the sky enveloped the scene within
    an elemental light. The thickening, varnishlike quality
of water in air, and heat—the pure clarity beginning to
    congeal—would capture this space at the edge of a village,
gathering its figures into one impression, while a fly ball
    hit long toward right center hung up against the base
of a cloud, the crowd rising to its feet as the runner on first
    broke joyously for second, toward home. Charles Boykin,
coming around the bases, grinned with the mouths of small boys
    under the tree, their biceps thicker as they looked at his.
So the game and those summers continued. But Charlie Justice
    played for the Redskins, his figure ghostly in the electronic
snow of T.V.—not on a field near the one that Willie
    Mozingo had plowed, before he took his chunky body into
far left field, a two-legged gleam in his cream-colored uniform,
    as afternoon deepened and the slanting sun made balls hard
to judge but he caught them anyway, back in the broom sedge.
    Fred Pittman signed the minor-league contract and people
went to Wilson to see him. The diamond was left to high-
    school games, to frog creak and owl whoop in midsummer
evenings, and the lightning bugs coming on in a space that
    held the stars. Houses in sight of the diamond oak
lit up their windows with the glow of T.V. Always a few
    farm boys, not risking injury, hit rocks toward the trees
with broomsticks, or prevailed on a younger brother to throw
    them one more pitch down the middle, so they could drive
the baseball over the weeded ditch, out of the pasture.

Wendell Berry

THE SYCAMORE
for Harry Caudill

In the place that is my own place, whose earth
I am shaped in and must bear, there is an old tree growing,
a great sycamore that is a wondrous healer of itself.
Fences have been tied to it, nails driven into it,
hacks and whittles cut in it, the lightning has burned it.
There is no year it has flourished in
that has not harmed it. There is a hollow in it
that is its death, though its living brims whitely
at the lip of the darkness and flows outward.
Over all its scars has come the seamless white
of the bark. It bears the gnarls of its history
healed over. It has risen to a strange perfection
in the warp and bending of its long growth.
It has gathered all accidents into its purpose.
It has become the intention and radiance of its dark fate.
It is a fact, sublime, mystical and unassailable.
In all the country there is no other like it.
I recognize in it a principle, an indwelling
the same as itself, and greater, that I would be ruled by.
I see that it stands in its place, and feeds upon it,
and is fed upon, and is native, and maker.

AIR AND FARE

From my wife and household and fields
that I have so carefully come to in my time
I enter the craziness of travel,
the reckless elements of air and fire.
Having risen up from my native land,
I find myself smiled at by beautiful women,
making me long for a whole life
to devote to each one, making love to her
in some house, in some way of sleeping
and waking I would make only for her.
And all over the country I find myself
falling in love with houses, woods, and farms
that I will never set foot in.
My eyes go wandering through America,
two wayfaring brothers, resting in silence
against the forbidden gates. O what if
an angel came to me, and said,
"Go free of what you have done. Take
what you want." The atoms of blood
and brain and bone strain apart
at the thought. What I am is the way home.
Like rest after a sleepless night,
my old love comes on me in midair.

HISTORY

for Wallace Stegner

1

The crops were made, the leaves
were down, three frosts had lain
upon the broad stone
step beneath the door;
as I walked away

the houses were shut, quiet
under their drifting smokes,
the women stooped at the hearths.
Beyond the farthest tracks
of any domestic beast
my way led me, into
a place for which I knew
no names. I went by paths
that bespoke intelligence
and memory I did not know.
Noonday held sounds of moving
water, moving air, enormous
stillness of old trees.
Though I was weary and alone,
song was near me then,
wordless and gay as a deer
lightly stepping. Learning
the landmarks and the ways
of that land, so I might
go back, if I wanted to,
my mind grew new, and lost
the backward way. I stood
at last, long hunter and child,
where this valley opened,
a word I seemed to know
though I had not heard it.
Behind me, along the crooks
and slants of my approach,
a low song sang itself,
as patient as the light.
On the valley floor the woods
grew rich: great poplars,
beeches, sycamores,
walnuts, sweet gums, lindens,
oaks. They stood apart
and open, the winter light
at rest among them. Yes,

and as I came down
I heard a little stream
pouring into the river.

   2

Since then I have arrived here
many times. I have come
on foot, on horseback, by boat,
and by machine—by earth,
water, air, and fire.
I came with axe and rifle.
I came with a sharp eye
and the price of land. I came
in bondage, and I came
in freedom not worth the name.
From the high outlook
of that first day I have come
down two hundred years
across the worked and wasted
slopes, by eroding tracks
of the joyless horsepower of greed.
Through my history's despite
and ruin, I have come
to its remainder, and here
have made the beginning
of a farm intended to become
my art of being here.
By it I would instruct
my wants: they should belong
to one another and to this place.
Until my song comes here
to learn its words, my art
is but the hope of song.

   3

All the lives this place
has had, I have. I eat

my history day by day.
Bird, butterfly, and flower
pass through the seasons of
my flesh. I dine and thrive
on offal and old stone,
and am combined within
the story of the ground.
By this earth's life, I have
its greed and innocence,
its violence, its peace.
Now let me feed my song
upon the life that is here
that is the life that is gone.
This blood has turned to dust
and liquefied again in stem
and vein ten thousand times.
Let what is in the flesh,
O Muse, be brought to mind.

STAY HOME

I will wait here in the fields
to see how well the rain
brings on the grass.
In the labor of the fields
longer than a man's life
I am at home. Don't come with me.
You stay home too.

I will be standing in the woods
where the old trees
move only with the wind
and then with gravity.
In the stillness of the trees

I am at home. Don't come with me.
You stay home too.

IN RAIN

1

I go in under foliage
light with rain-light
in the hill's cleft,
and climb, my steps
silent as flight
on the wet leaves.
Where I go, stones
are wearing away
under the sky's flow.

2

The path I follow
I can hardly see
it is so faintly trod
and overgrown.
At times, looking,
I fail to find it
among dark trunks, leaves
living and dead. And then
I am alone, the woods
shapeless around me.
I look away, my gaze
at rest among leaves,
and then I see the path
again, a dark way going
on through the light.

3

In a mist of light
falling with the rain

I walk this ground
of which dead men
and women I have loved
are part, as they
are part of me. In earth,
in blood, in mind,
the dead and living
into each other pass,
as the living pass
in and out of loves
as stepping to a song.
The way I go is
marriage to this place,
grace beyond chance,
love's braided dance
covering the world.

4

Marriages to marriages
are joined, husband and wife
are plighted to all
husbands and wives,
any life has all lives
for its delight.
Let the rain come,
the sun, and then the dark,
for I will rest
in an easy bed tonight.

Fred Chappell

REMEMBERING WIND MOUNTAIN AT SUNSET

Off Hurricane Creek where
the heady rattlers even the loggers
abash, out of Sandy
Mush and Big Laurel and
Greasy Branch, off the hacksaw edge of Freeze Land,
those winds huddle in the notch
atop Wind Mountain, where counties Madison
and Buncombe meet but never join.
Hardscrabble Aeolus,
that stir of zephyrs is the sigh of poor
folk screwed in between the rocks up
Meadow Fork and Sugar Camp and Trust, Luck,
Sliding Knob, and Bluff.
A lean wind and a meat-snatcher. Wind
full of hopeless bones.

High on Wind Mountain I heard
from the valley below
the wearied-to-silence lamentation of busted hands,
busted spines, galled mules and horses, last breeze
rubbing the raw board-edge of the corncrib,
whimper of cold green beans in a cube of fat,
the breathing of clay-colored feet unhooked
from iron brogans.
A glinty small miasma

rises off the rocks in the cornfield.
the cowbell dwindles
toward dusk.

I went walking up Chunky Gal
To watch the blackbird whup the owl.

Friend, you who sit where some money is,
I tell you, Sometimes the poor are
poor in spirit, the wind is robbing
them of breath
of life, wind from always Somewhere Else,
directionless unfocused desire,
but driving the young ones like thistle seed
toward Pontiac, Detroit, Cincinnati,
Somewhere, wherever is money,
out of the hills.
Can't make a go
in bloody Madison, too much the rocks
and thickety briars suck the breath of the hand.
Suck the womenfolk to twig-and-twine
limberjacks, suck the puckered houses sad,
tumbly shack by blackberry wilderness
fills to the ridgepole with copperhead
and sawbriar. The abandoned smokehouse
droops, springhouse hoards dead leaves.

I see blackbird fighting the crow
But I know something he don't know.

Over Hunger Cove
the rain-crow keeps conjuring rain
till Shitbritches Creek is flooded, tobacco
drowned this year one more year,
the township of Marshall bets half its poke
and the French Broad takes it
with a murmur of thunder.

Lord, let these sawtooth tops
let me breathe, give me one good stand
of anything but elderbush and milkweed,
I'll keep Mama's Bible dusted off,
I'll try not to murder
for spite nor even for money,
just let that wind hush
its bones a little and not fly so hard
at the barn roof and the
halfbuilt haystack, I'll go to the Singing
on the Mountain with Luramae this
time I swear I will.

Fished up Bear Creek till I was half dead.
Caught a pound of weeds and a hornyhead.

Where you're from's
Hanging Dog, ain't it, boy I knowed
your daddy years back, that was your Uncle
Lige wasn't it lost his arm at
the old Caldwell sawmill, they called him Sawmill
after, took to hunting sang
and medicine root, heard old Lige had died,
is that the truth, I disremember, he
was how old? Hundred and forty-nine
counting nights and hard knocks,
that's what he told me, I'll never forget.
Standing right there by that stove he said it.

If you could eat the wind,
if you could chew it and swallow
it for strength like a windmill.
If anything could be made of this wind in
winter with its scythes of ice when it comes dragging
blue snow over the ridgetops and down
the mountainsides here to the house, finds any
little cranny, wind squirms through the holes

like an army of squirrels.
Go over and sit by the fire, won't
be long till your fingers turn blue again
anyhow. Somehow
I don't have my proper strength
a-winters, been to the doc how many times,
it's a poser to him says he, I told him
Doc I just get down weak as rag soup and
he says, Maybe you need a rest, By God
rest I says, reckon maybe I do,
why don't I lay up here for a while.

I saw blackbird fighting the hawk,
He whupped his hiney with a pokeweed stalk.

And then he says, Now how you
going to pay me? I says, Pay you doc, you'll just
have to garnisheer them Rest Wages.

Two women fighting over a box of snuff,
Lost three tits before they had enough.

First snow like a sulphate powder, bluish,
and up-top the trees like frozen lace, crystal white
against the crystal blue of morning north,
look fragile as tinsel, no wind yet much,
only down the back of your neck now and again to
remind you how long about milking
time it'll come on.
It'll come, everything hurtful will come on.
Here is the place where pain is born.
No salve or balm.
Ever you notice how deep cold the rocks get?
No I mean it, you hoeing round in the field
summertime, hit rocks, sparks
jumping every whichway, come winter
you can beat all day on a rock with a crowbar,

never see spark one, rocks
get froze up deep in the heart is why, told
my oldest boy, No wonder our raggedy
ass is cold, even the goddam rocks
have done give up.

                  And if you was to get
a little warm, go in by the cookstove there,
just makes it worse, wind when
you go out peels the feeling-warm right
off, you'll think you've fell
in Spring Creek River, way it goes over you
ice water, but the funny part is, come summer
same wind out of the same place,
feels like it's pouring out of a coalstove,
ain't a breath of soothe in it. Now that's funny.

Maybe the wind like that gets me so low.
Hateful to think of it stepping on my grave
when I'm took off, and then still clawing
you know the apple tree
and the hayfield and the roof of this house,
still clawing
at my young ones after I'm laid safe
out of it. What's the relief in that?
Under the sod you know here'll
come that Freeze Land wind crawling my joints.

Turkey buzzard took old blackbird flying
Like a pissant riding on a dandelion.

Youngish preacherman, heard him
say they ain't no bad without some good
in it somewhere, wanted
to ask him, What's the good in poison oak,
tell me because I can raise twenty solid acres
right in a jiffy, sawbriar too, didn't think

what was the good of this Freeze Land wind, you
know it gets so much inside you, never think
about it being anything, I mean
nothing, just there is all, not anything.
Something you can't see like that you never think.
Like that War in Europe, what'd I know
back here in the stump roots, but they stuck
me over there in the mud
till wild rose and ragweed took my bottom land.

For fighting niggers and hauling loads,
Pulled fifteen months on the county roads.

Friend, you who sit
in the vale of comfort,
consider if you will that there are corners
in this flab land where shale edge
of hunger is chipping out
hearts for weapons, man don't
look from year to year but day by day
alone, suffering of flesh
is whetting the knife edge of spirit in
lower Appalachia, margins
where no one thinks you're his buddy,
don't come driving that big-ass Lincoln
up Hogback Ridge if you like your paint job,
they's some old
bushy boys in here kill a man for
a quarter, eyegod, you seen about that feller
in the papers? I'm not saying
what I've heard about them Henson brothers,
you knowed old man Henson or your daddy did,
him that burned the sheriff
out, had two boys nigh
as lowdown as ever he was, I
don't know what-all I've heard tell.

Up on Wind Mountain there ain't no help.
Blackbird went and killed hisself.

Friend, sit tight on your money,
what you've got, there's a man
on a mountain thinks he needs it worse.

All this I heard in the stir
of wind-quarrel in Wind Mountain notch,
rich tatters of speech
of poor folk drifting like bright Monarchs.
And then on the breeze a cowbell,
and the kitchen lights went on in the valley below,
and a lonesome churchbell
calling
home, home, home, home
till I could bear it no more.
Turned my back.
Walked down the mountain's other side.

They hauled old blackbird's carcass away,
Buried him head-down-deep in red clay.

Here comes the preacher to say the last word:
"It's a fitten end for old blackbird."

ABANDONED SCHOOLHOUSE
ON LONG BRANCH

The final scholar scrawls his long
Black name in aisle dust, licks the air
With his inquisitive double tongue,
Coils up in shadow of a broken chair

And dozes like the farmer boys
Who never learned the capital
Of Idaho, found out the joys
Of long division, or learned what all

Those books were all about. Most panes
Are missing; the web-milky windows
Are open to the world. Dust grains
Swirl up and show which way the wind blows.

K. B. + R. J., cut deep
In a childish heart on the cloakroom wall.
Now Roger and Katherine Johnson sleep
Long past the summons of the morning bell.

The teacher sleeps narrow too, on yonder
Side of Sterling Mountain, as stern
With her fate as with a loutish blunder
In a Bible verse she'd set them to learn.

Sunset washes the blackboard. Bees
Return to the fluent attic nest
Where much is stored. Their vocalese
Soothes the patient golden dust.

Kelly Cherry

ON WATCHING A YOUNG MAN
PLAY TENNIS

The male poets run, lifting their feet like pros.
Others fish, and then there are those
Whose driving force
Sends them to the sandtraps of an eighteen-hole course

In search of metaphor. I have no yen
For sun and sky and earth, no kin-
Ship for the sea.
The element of mind is quite enough for me,

And dreaming in the damp of poolside shade,
I let imagination wade
Through the shallow
Stretch of time beyond a bend of tanning elbow,

And burning thigh, to where the poet plays
A love game with my yesterdays.
I have no zest
For exercise, no yearning after limberness

For the sake of limb alone, but enjoy,
Girlishly, this energy of Boy
That seeks to know
The meaning of *mens sana in corpore sano.*

Turning on my side, I see the shadow
Of his racket on the court grow
Long and widen
Till its very silence trespasses on the Haydn

Which carries from the house, and I put down
My drink and move inside where sound
And light and drift
Of dinner's smells serve, albeit fleetingly, to lift

My spirits to a plane of praise upon
Which I can stand and frankly own
That I am tired,
And lazy, and will leave to others more inspired

The satisfaction of the outdoor sports.
A young man in his tennis shorts
Suffices to
Realign the balance of my brain and back so

That I am paralyzed with memory
Of verse and versifier. (Yet I
Remember when
I volleyed more than words with the artfullest of men.)

HOW TO WAIT

First things first: dig in at the lake's edge.
Use sedge for your rug;
sleep on a stone ledge.

No phonographs needed here—
the music you hear is made by a dozen soft tongues
lapping water, by a hungry lion,
deer.

Sun brands your shoulders;
you are singled out for life
by this indelible contact.

Yes, you might as well face facts.
The eyes see you,
the men pity you.
The animals would like to devour you.
No one will save you.

You live by the lake, waiting.
Things to do:

For supper, suck the meat
from a crayfish, or chew watery plants,
spitting out what you can't eat—
it'll feed the white ants
fumbling at your feet.

When the moon comes up, look by its light
for changes—the mountains that move
nearer, the sky that drops,
trees that shed their bark and grow into giants overnight—

The next day, rain.

Locate a thicket to hide in.
Before you enter, make sure it's empty.
That commotion? A cricket.

All day you wait.

You are so damp that beans sprout from your skin,
flowers from your fingertips.
You are budding; open
your mouth to fate

and take it in—
those lips are already smeary with sin.

Generously flick seeds aside.

Grow in the ground; become one
with earth and sun.

Surrender yourself. Evaporate. Abide.

THE ROSE

A botanical lecture

It's the cup of blood,
the dark drink lovers sip,
the secret food

It's the pulse and elation
of girls on their birthdays,
it's good-byes at the railroad station

It's the murmur of rain,
the blink of daylight
in a still garden, the clink
of crystal; later, the train

pulling out, the white cloth,
apples, pears, and champagne—
good-bye! good-bye!
We'll weep petals, and dry
our tears with thorns

A steep country springs up beyond
the window, with a sky like a pond,

a flood. It's a rush
of bright horror, a burning bush,
night's heart,
the living side of the holy rood

It's the whisper of grace in the martyrs' wood

IN THE GARDEN BY THE SEA: EASTER

These giant grape hyacinths
Rise like porticoes from stems like plinths,
Flinging their fragrance

On the April air.
Something *is* everywhere,
Something like air

Or God, is there where you thought
There was nothing, not
Anything, where matter, caught

And stuck
On a hook,
Squirms and is eaten, solider than any book

A writer ever wrote.
Something exists that is not merely of note,
Something unwritten but wrought

In sense and dimension,
Something like an ocean,
Say, or the moment of bright tension

Before the body gives
Itself to the idea that it lives
And is loved and loves and grieves

For the incommunicant,
Whom nothing touches
And something can't.

WAITING FOR THE END OF TIME

Behind the window, in that room where rain
And wind were instrumentalists playing
On the windowpane, you were asleep, again,
And never heard the words that I was saying.
I didn't say them for you to hear, I said
Them to your heart, that listening, third ear.

What anyone's heart knows is what has been bled
Out of it. . . .

      It's February, a different year,
And spring seems something that a season might do
For the sheer delight of being sprung,
A kind of rhythm, a heartbeat, or *parlando*
(The words are spoken even though they're sung),
And everything is different now, except
Time itself, which goes right on being kept.

FOR TEEN-AGE BOYS MURDERED IN TEXAS:
THE REFUSAL TO DRAMATIZE BLOODLUST

This once we will vanquish violence,
stake the heart & cross
the spirit's path

so it won't rise, that godawful
gorge hot & grainy
moving against the constricted throat

This once we will forgo
theater (that's
tribute from a poet,

ask Dickey or Bly)
I tell you
27 children is reason enough

to burn certain books,
go outside,
see how the sky looks

when day breaks thru
O creeping mist of the midnight unspeakable, lie
still upon the lilies & dissolve

James Dickey

HUNTING CIVIL WAR RELICS AT NIMBLEWILL CREEK

As he moves the mine detector
A few inches over the ground,
Making it vitally float
Among the ferns and weeds,
I come into this war
Slowly, with my one brother,
Watching his face grow deep
Between the earphones,
For I can tell
If we enter the buried battle
Of Nimblewill
Only by his expression.

Softly he wanders, parting
The grass with a dreaming hand.
No dead cry yet takes root
In his clapped ears
Or can be seen in his smile.
But underfoot I feel
The dead regroup,
The burst metals all in place,
The battle lines be drawn
Anew to include us
In Nimblewill,
And I carry the shovel and pick

More as if they were
Bright weapons that I bore.
A bird's cry breaks
In two, and into three parts.
We cross the creek; the cry
Shifts into another,
Nearer, bird, and is
Like the shout of a shadow—
Lived-with, appallingly close—
Or the soul, pronouncing
"Nimblewill":
Three tones; your being changes.

We climb the bank;
A faint light glows
On my brother's mouth.
I listen, as two birds fight
For a single voice, but he
Must be hearing the grave,
In pieces, all singing
To his clamped head,
For he smiles as if
He rose from the dead within
Green Nimblewill
And stood in his grandson's shape.

No shot from the buried war
Shall kill me now,
For the dead have waited here
A hundred years to create
Only the look on the face
Of my one brother,
Who stands among them, offering
A metal dish
Afloat in the trembling weeds,
With a long-buried light on his lips

At Nimblewill
And the dead outsinging two birds.

I choke the handle
Of the pick, and fall to my knees
To dig wherever he points,
To bring up mess tin or bullet,
To go underground
Still singing, myself,
Without a sound,
Like a man who renounces war,
Or one who shall lift up the past,
Not breathing "Father,"
At Nimblewill,
But saying, "Fathers! Fathers!"

SNOW ON A SOUTHERN STATE

Alongside the train I labor
To change wholly into my spirit,
As the place of my birth falls upward

Into the snow,
And my pale, sealed face looks in
From the world where it ripples and sails,
Sliding through culverts,

Plunging through tunnels while flakes
Await my long, streaming return
As they wait for this country to rise

And become something else in mid-air.
With a just-opened clicking, I come
Forth into fresh, buried meadows
Of muffled night light

Where people still sit on their porches
Screened in for eternal summer,
Watching the snow

Like grated shadow sift
Impossibly to them.
Through the window I tell them dumbly
That the snow is like

A man, stretched out upon landscape
And a spotless berth,
Who is only passing through

Their country, who means no harm:
Who stares in distrust at his ghost
Also flying, feet first, through the distance.
Numbly, the lips of his spirit

Move, and a fur-bearing steeple looms up
Through the heart of his mirrored breast.
The small town where he was born

Assembles around it,
The neon trying, but obviously unreal,
The parked cars clumsily letting
Pureness, a blinding burden,

Come slowly upon them.
All are still, all are still,
For the breath-holding window and I

Only must move through the silence,
Bearing my huge, prone ghost
Up, out, and now flying over
The vapor-lamp-glowing high school

Into the coming fields
Like a thing we cannot put down.
Yet the glass gives out of my image

And the laid clicking dies, as the land
All around me shines with the power
Of renewing my youth
By changing the place where I lived it.

There is nothing here, now, to watch
The bedclothes whirl into flakes.
What should be warm in these blankets

Has powdered down into its own
Steel-blue and feathery visions
Of weddings opposed by the world:
Is hovering over

A dead cotton field, which awaits
Its touch as awaiting completion:
Is building the pinewoods again

For this one night of their lives:
With the equilibrium
Of bones, is falling, falling,
Falling into the river.

IN THE MARBLE QUARRY

    Beginning to dangle beneath
The wind that blows from the undermined wood,
    I feel the great pulley grind,

    The thread I cling to lengthen
And let me soaring and spinning down into marble,
    Hooked and weightlessly happy

    Where the squared sun shines
Back equally from all four sides, out of stone
    And years of dazzling labor,

To land at last among men
Who cut with power saws a Parian whiteness
And, chewing slow tobacco,

Their eyebrows like frost,
Shunt house-sized blocks and lash them to cables
And send them heavenward

Into small-town banks,
Into the columns and statues of government buildings,
But mostly graves.

I mount my monument and rise
Slowly and spinningly from the white-gloved men
Toward the hewn sky

Out of the basement of light,
Sadly, lifted through time's blinding layers
On perhaps my tombstone

In which the original shape
Michelangelo believed was in every rock upon earth
Is heavily stirring,

Surprised to be an angel,
To be waked in North Georgia by the ponderous play
Of men with ten-ton blocks

But no more surprised than I
To feel sadness fall off as though I myself
Were rising from stone

Held by a thread in midair,
Badly cut, local-looking, and totally uninspired,
Not a masterwork

Or even worth seeing at all
But the spirit of this place just the same,
Felt here as joy.

AT DARIEN BRIDGE

The sea here used to look
As if many convicts had built it,

Standing deep in their ankle chains,
Ankle-deep in the water, to smite

The land and break it down to salt,
I was in this bog as a child

When they were all working all day
To drive the pilings down.

I thought I saw the still sun
Strike the side of a hammer in flight

And from it a sea bird be born
To take off over the marshes.

As the gray climbs the side of my head
And cuts my brain off from the world,

I walk and wish mainly for birds,
For the one bird no one has looked for

To spring again from a flash
Of metal, perhaps from the scratched

Wedding band on my ring finger.
Recalling the chains of their feet,

I stand and look out over grasses
At the bridge they built, long abandoned,

Breaking down into water at last,
And long, like them, for freedom

Or death, or to believe again
That they worked on the ocean to give it

The unchanging, hopeless look
Out of which all miracles leap.

George Garrett

OLD SLAVEMARKET: ST. AUGUSTINE, FLA.

Beneath the fort where Osceola starved
and armored ghosts of Spaniards prowl
for the improbable fountain, a green park,
where this museum piece is standing still

in good repair, is scene of crime.
There, grinning to gloss a savage text,
pale tourists pose and photograph, unvexed
by shady aftertime.

The seabreeze troubles these rich palms
hardly at all. The light that shone
on all our naked fathers will not burn again.

But Truth, distorted, yowls for alms.
Do not go deep, or rotten bones,
yanked into view, will shriek in pain.

RUGBY ROAD

In memory of Hyam Plutzik

1
My days, these days, begin on a road called Rugby,
a rich name summoning counterfeit ivy and distant towers

and the loud cries of far-off playing fields
where all the young men, being English
belabor each other in impeccable English
while swans go by like a snowy procession of Popes.

O far from Rugby Road!
Far too from all the sweat and blood,
the grunt and groan and scrimmage of a burly game.

My days begin on Rugby Road
where first light blesses everything
with promises not a living soul will keep.

Now I walk past lawns and houses.
And I in turn am passed by
            by station wagons,
each awiggle with cargo of kids,
each one driven by the same housewife.
She wears a formal painted mask
somewhere between the expressions
of comedy and tragedy.

Ah, lady, I have seen
your nightgown dancing
on the clothesline round with wind.
I have danced with your empty nightgown.
I have hoisted it for my sail
and voyaged like a pirate far and wide,
a fool on the Ship of Fools.
I publish no secrets because
I know only my own.

Now stands above an intricate corner
Mr. Jefferson's splendid imitation of
the Pantheon, here called the Rotunda
and used (the old joke goes)
exclusively for a Rotunda.

I walk through the stain of that shadow
and down the colonnade of Mr. Jefferson's Lawn
and finally meet Mr. Jefferson himself,
seated, wearing a pensive, studious look,
expensive eighteenth-century clothes,
and an excellent patina.

Beneath his gaze, boys in coats and ties
go to and from classes, carrying books,
the weight of all our wisdom in their hands.

I think of Jefferson, the eccentric,
dabbler, gadgeteer and dilettante
high in his crazy castle, Monticello,
which time has also dignified.

A radical who rocked the boat,
who dumped King George and all his tea
into an indifferent sea.

A virtuoso who could turn
pomp and circumstance into a circus tune.
Who tamed and whipped the Lion through hoops of fire.

Time which will tame us one and all,
which can turn love songs into howls,
may yet make music of my groans
or teach me how to sit up and to beg.

   2

I am thinking today of the death of a friend,
a poet, a scholar and a Jew
from whom a Christian gentleman could learn
some charity. I have the news today
that he is dead. "He was in great pain,
but brave until the very last
when his mind wandered."

Where does the mind wander?

Do we go all naked and alone
when flesh and worn-out senses fail?
Or are we at last tailored in radiance,
wearing smiles like an absolute shoeshine?

I dream a playing field, all green and Greek,
where plump, conventional nymphs and satyrs roam
and romp with only sunlight for clothing.
(O far from Rugby Road!)

But you, I believe, have found at last
the ruined wall in a dusty place
and kneel there praying for us now.
I would join you there if I dared.

Your prayers are only songs.
Those songs become birds and fly
over the wall and into a sudden garden
where trees are dreaming and fountains play
a bloodless, sweatless game of light and air.

And there one day a bird will sing your name
and fountains begin to dance to that new tune
like young girls veiled in moonbeams.

That shade is far too subtle for my mind.
I do not want to die. I fear
my flesh will make me scream before
it lets me wander where I will.

Better to be a bronze imposter.
Better to wear a coat and tie
and babble of green Greek fields.
Better to hold wisdom in one hand.

I fear I can never make old stones sing.
I fear to leave flesh and bones behind.
I have forgotten how to say my prayers.

3

In the halls my colleagues hurry
to classes, conferences, coffee,
all to the tune of ringing bells.
Bells toll to celebrate beginning and the end
of every fifty-minute session where

we deal out knowledge like a pack of cards.
Perhaps we should wear a cap and bells,
belled mortarboards in honor of
a perilous, ridiculous vocation.

there are no bells in that garden
and the leaves of the trees are laughter

We fear the ridiculous more
than a cage full of lions and tigers.

How can a mind begin to wander free
until at last the last pride of the flesh
falls away like a sad fig leaf?

Leaves are falling here and now
to be raked and turned into smoke.

your fountains are vague as the smoke
and the leaves of the trees are laughter
and the birds in the leaves are songs
and the fruit of the trees is sweet
            and good to eat

Here in a hall the typewriters chatter,
crickets calling in the language of crickets.

And here the unwandering mortal mind
leaps like a grasshopper, tense and agile,
from one blade of grass to another
on the barbered space we call The Lawn.

Some of us are gathering grapes from thistles
and some are busy baking stones for bread.
Our elders doze and yawn like sheiks,
propped on the pillows of reputation.
"Sir, have you seen Susanna lately?
In secret places have you seen
Wisdom, Sapientia, pale Diana,
white and bare as the winter moon?"
They wink and will not answer.

The young lions roar and jump through hoops.
There is a game like rugby going on,
grunts and groans in impeccable English.

4

I envy your open weather, Mr. Jefferson,
the rain and shine, the simple pleasure of
a uniform of painless bronze.
Your words endure in marble places.

I honor you, my dead and buried friend,
whose words exist in slender volumes.

Behind the words the song and dance is free,
free like the birds to fly south from the snow.
South to islands, the richest islands,
where our suntans will be tuxedos,
where girls the color of milk and honey
dance and the breeze is French perfume
and the surf is orchids and ermine
and the roughest blanket is the moonlight.

A bell sounds like a bugle.
I must try to muster my wandering mind.

They are burning up the leaves.
They are burning up the typewriters.
They are folding up their silken tents.

I light a cigarette and reach for a book.
I straighten my tie and grit my teeth
in what I hope and trust will pass
for a polite, uncertain grin.

FOR A BITTER SEASON

The oak tree in my front yard dies,
whose leaves are sadder than cheap wrapping paper,
and nothing I can do will keep it long.

Last spring in another place a pear tree
glistened in bloom like a graceful drift of snow.
Birds and bees loved that spacious white

and a daughter was born in the time of flowers.

Now I am a stranger and my oak tree dies
young. Blight without a name, a bad omen.
I die, too, fret in my familiar flesh,

and I take this for a bitter season.
We have lived too long with fear. We take
fear for granted like a drunken uncle,

like a cousin not quite all there
who's always there. I have lived too long
with the stranger who haunts my mirror.

Night in the city and the sirens scream
fresh disasters for my morning paper.
The oak tree in the front yard dies.

Bless us, a houseful of loving strangers,
one good woman, two small boys, a man
waking from sleep to cough his name.

And bless my daughter made of snow and bluest eyes.

Andrew Hudgins

FLAMINGOS HAVE ARRIVED IN ASHTABULA

Flamingos have arrived in Ashtabula.
Or one has. Bending to fetch the morning paper,
the mayor saw it standing on her lawn,
poised one-legged like a plastic bird
jabbed in the grass, and thinking it a joke,
she laughed. It lumbered, lurched into the air
and sailed across her back fence, rising pink
against the near-pink Ashtabula dawn.

Flamingos have arrived in Ashtabula,
blown here we think by a line of thunderstorms
—a scrap of pink confetti on the wind—
except those storms were months ago. No zoo
reports a lost flamingo, and it doesn't seem lost.
It circles the airport tower, lands on the courthouse,
and stalks a drainage ditch behind the mall,
where people linger with binoculars
to watch a flamingo feed in Ashtabula.

A local bar, once Dewey's Hometown Lounge,
is now The Pink Flamingo—pink chairs, pink drinks.
Stuck in the ceiling, hundreds of plastic pink
flamingos hang over us upside down, observing,
while we sip pink gin and ponder the waitresses'
pink T-shirts. From them, even pinker pink

flamingos with sequin eyes return our gaze.
Flamingos have arrived in Ashtabula.

The tropical bodies resplendent against gray sky,
the languid beating of long wings—
we see them in our imagining and dreams, and now
in daylight we scan the sky, the bogs, the ditches
for a hint of pink or parrot-green, a red
that shimmers. Turquoise. Electric yellow eyes.
Or I do. I speak for no one but myself.
Flamingos have arrived in Ashtabula.

SOUTHERN LITERATURE

She hunched in the back seat, and fired
one Lucky off the one before.
She talked about her good friend Bill.
No one wrote like Bill anymore.

When the silence grew uncomfortable,
she'd count out my six rumpled ones,
and ask, *noblesse oblige,* "How ah
your literary lucubrations

progressing?" "Not good," I'd snarl. My poems
were going nowhere, like me—raw,
twenty-eight, and having, she said,
a worm's-eye view of life. And awe—

I had no sense of awe. But once
I lied, "Terrific! *The Atlantic*
accepted five." She smiled benignly,
composed and gaily fatalistic,

as I hammered to Winn-Dixie, revving
the slant six till it bucked and sputtered.
She smoothed her blue unwrinkled dress.
"Bill won the Nobel Prize," she purred.

If I laid rubber to the interstate,
and started speeding, how long, I wondered,
how long would she scream before she prayed?
Would she sing before I murdered her?

Would we make Memphis or New Orleans?
The world was gorgeous now, and bigger.
I reached for the gun I didn't own.
I chambered awe. I pulled the trigger.

THE HAWK ABOVE THE HOUSE

The hawk hung low above the house,
appraising:
        prey or not
              prey? Not.
Then it swung up, veered eastward—gone.
That moment
        I too ached to open
my great imagined wings, and arc
against the sun's arc, reversing it
and following its bright track back
through dawns and darkness
                till I soared
in sunlight above the stucco box
I sat on as a boy
        and there
I'd fold those gold imagined wings,
plummet, and from
          my father's roof
I'd watch the boy who watched for me.

O, he'd have given anything
to fly: the hawk
                exploding on
the sparrow or the sparrow,
                            frantic,
threading through the black-green cedars.
He'd have given anything to fly,
the rapt boy
                staring at the air,
imagining if he could imagine
hawk thought,
                deciding no, then knowing
it was impossible, a pure
extension of himself to wings
and cold predation,
                    he tried—and failed,
but not
        completely, as he had thought,
and here I am to tell him so.

A FLAG OF HONEYSUCKLE

From the brush pile I wrestled brittle limbs
and shoved
                them in the chipper. As I worked down
the six-month pile, a thin
                        green flag sprang up—
a slip of honeysuckle. I tugged
                            it; it
resisted,
            white threads infiltrating dark earth
—and suddenly I was on the Burlington
Street bridge in Iowa, watching
                            a cottonwood.
Spring floods had flushed it from the riverbank

and trundled it down river till it snagged.
Its leaves,
            fed by the heavy river, drooped,
drooped in the June, July, and August heat,
but held their ashen green,
                        and from the bridge
I conjured with the possibilities:
I am the tree. I am uprooted, adrift.
I made the world a tool
                  for my crude use.
It's how I've lived when I have had to, slapping
one feeble, transitory understanding
before another—
            each meaning a restive step
from what I was to what I hoped to be
—remarried? out of debt?—arriving now
at now: remarried,
                  paid, and contemplating
a ratty flag of green that waves its standard
above my brush.
            Rebirth? The weak
                        triumphant?
Blind nature? They rise
                  so easily to mind
without the force of need to make me fight them,
old friends
            returning from old understandings,
whipping this twig of honeysuckle into fragrance.

THE CHINABERRY TREES

. . . and oh, the chinaberry trees in niggertown!
            —E. Welty to K. A. Porter, 1941

Under the flowering chinaberry
we parked, closed our dull eyes,

55

and scent absorbed us in a world
midnight intensifies.

We gave ourselves to fragrance, eyes shut
to barrel fires, and wicks
flickering in smoky shacks.
What was there to fix

our eyes on—purple flowers hidden
in the leaves and the leaves in darkness?
We didn't have to understand
what we have witnessed. Fragrance

numbed and suspended us among
then-the-past and then-
the-future, and then, which was the now
we levitated in.

I've never been so far transported,
as I am there, under trees
I wouldn't have on my green lawn.
By May, the fetid berries

rot in the hot shade underneath
the lowest branches. Crows
riot in the reeking poison,
not harmful to them of course—

shrieking like Furies in the fruit,
mating and making mess.
Azalea, redbud, cherry grace
our lawns. On March nights, thus,

we nose our cars past barbecue
and juke joints. We park outside
tilted shotgun shacks, eyes closed,
and breathe deep, nullified,

releasing ourselves to perfume, knowledge
out of context, abstraction
our talking can't diminish. We live
in the pilfered Indian

gift of the chinaberry—the tree
uprooted from my lawn
but thriving there in niggertown,
lush and left alone.

When a gray battered truck scraped past,
we awakened, blinking. Once,
thrilling us, a pistol shot rang out,
and after, in the silence,

a raw harmonica exploded,
someone's ridicule
sucked backward through the instrument
the laughter lurid, cruel,

and magnified to frightening music—
except we weren't afraid
or chastened. We reveled in its rage,
and hung on its harsh fading.

Next spring we'll drive there once again.
In darkness we'll drift free,
and open ourselves to opening
under the chinaberry.

THE YOUNG OAKS

In rose and gold declining light,
I'm not what I'd foreseen.

I grasp a lanky water oak.
Embracing it, I lean

into it, sway, and yield myself
to its limber stem. Then, looser,
I pull and push, grappling in rapture
with my rough young seducer.

Fourteen feet tall, thick as a my arm,
and sprightly, it pushes back.
It loves a tussle! Sap wells up
through river, riverbank,

taproot, and trunk—and into me.
I tingle, toe to crown,
and soon I launch out, swing and sway,
bending the young tree down

in graceless dancing till it springs
and flips me to the grass.
I rise, take hold once more, and wrestle
till the virtues of it pass

from the oak to me. Or we exchange:
the oak absorbs my aches,
ungracious glooms, leakages
and lethargy. Twelve oaks

cavort before me as I shout
a young man's song, and lash
my gray skin scarlet with a branch
I've broken from an ash.

I pat the oak, mutter good-bye.
—embarrassed now, and brusque—
and limp home but less painfully
in the rose and pale gold dusk.

T. R. Hummer

THE ANTICHRIST IN ARKANSAS

At the edge of town, daylilies the gold of old whiskey
Move tonelessly. At the margin of the courthouse shadow,
A little sky gives off its one unchanging line.
It is written in the Gnostic *Gospel of Truth* that life is nightmare,
As if people were murdering them, though there is no one
Even pursuing them, or they themselves are killing
Their neighbors, for they have been stained with their blood.
Let there be a little clarity here, let the light arrive,
The way the dynamite train rolls into Arkadelphia:
An overwhelming ablution, a scheduled breakdown.
In the crib behind the cotton gin, three of them are gathered.
In the alley off Jefferson Street, they are giving secret signs.
Who are they? Call them the Brotherhood of Darkness.
Give them emblems: khaki workshirts, Prince Albert in a can.
They live in clapboard temples set up in the taboo precincts,
They worship at the Synagogues of the Flesh of the Holy Pig.
Mornings, hours before sunrise, they kneel at the open flame;
Past midnight, if you wake in an impure sweat, you can hear
Their pentatonic psalms sift through the veils of the juke joints.
You who are uninitiate, you who walk the sunlit bricks
Of the Main Street sidewalk past the bank to the hotel café,
You of the regimental necktie, you who render
Unto Woodrow Wilson, live in the obvious houses,
Drive Fords, dance to "Arkansas Traveler"—Brotherhood of Light,
You think the fields at least are innocent, gathered without

The rhetoric of pastoral, the flat farmland, the plows
Moving in the middle distance; you believe at least
In the trees, gone in their green brooding. But in 1919,
83 bodies were given to druid oaks on the fringes
Of these blesséd little cities: Conway, Fort Smith, Fayetteville,
West Memphis, El Dorado, Pine Bluff, Forrest City,
The mecca of Hot Springs. How many know
The ritual formula that exorcises unclean flesh?
How many have learned the arcana, the knotting
And unknotting of hemp? So it has been written
In *The Paraphrase of Shem,* and quoted
In *The Arkansas Gazette: Nature turned her dark vagina*
And cast from her the power of fire, which was in her
From the beginning, through the practice of darkness.
Look: already the evening brightens, already the locomotive
Crosses the valley in a shimmer of pure entropic heat.
Everything in the flesh converges. In a moment it will be too late.
Gather them up, believer. Put them on the backs of mules.
Take them where the wind completes its broken sentence
Of damnation against the elder, against the ash.
The secret is simplicity: pray to me, the spirit who steals
The breath of the one whose feet no longer touch
The ground; make sacrifice to the god who silences him
Whose testicles bleed in his own unsanctified mouth.

PLATE GLASS

for Edward Hirsch and after Barthelme

Over this city of transparent buildings, the zodiac staggers, bombed
On mercury and the vapors of naphthalene. One more unimaginable
Down-And-Out Year Of Our Lord has come and gone
When Houston, Texas, tossed its crutch and limped toward heaven
In robes of polyester and rhinestone, still unhealed.
The melancholy that rises now from the entropy of the Cotton Exchange
Is worthy of the brilliant self-indulgence of a Keats.

But that woman on the avenue is the cropduster's lover. She believes
In a universe the size of the palm of a hand, worlds you can snuff
With a single gesture, like the sun. She has flown in a yellow biplane,
Trailing clouds of herbicide, occluding malls, galleries
Of overpriced landscapes, tiny refineries. Her pilot tied down the stick
With binder-twine and scrambled to the forward cockpit
Where she waited with her blouse undone for the password
To the city physic and the city psychic, the *genius loci* of the vision
Of street-sweepers and seraphim, *gnosis* at 6000 feet.
From where she hovered, ghettos appeared vivid as needlepoint.
The ruined shack where Lightnin' Hopkins was born assumed
The lineaments of a tragic miniature, the detail of fine cloisonné.
Architects who stood on the sixtieth crystal floor of Mobil Oil
Watching her loop and roll into the æther of the profit margin
Suddenly realized transcendence is of point of view. In a flash,
They understood how, for centuries, the thunderheads were changing
From spirit to water, from hurricane to distillate of acid, an image
With multiple forms in the light. But here and now she stops like anyone
On the sidewalk in front of a Neiman-Marcus window
Under the blinding Texas sun, staring in at priceless platinum
Corkscrews, the metal still burning from the crucible and the anvil,
At laser-powered toasters, holographic lingerie, his-and-her
Sports cars with windshields deadened the gray of lead alkali.
Beside them, she recognizes a perfect scale model of Houston
Crafted of resonate crystal calcite and carved dry ice
Whose CO_2 vapors rise heavenward in polarized mimesis
Of fluorocarbon haze, a shimmer of argon and Treflan.
She tries to make out a tiny image of herself on the sidewalk
In front of plate glass, staring in, trying to discover an even smaller self
Staring farther in—but there is only absence where she thinks she is,
Regression, inviolate light. She believes it could be simpler than it is
To know the real, if only the names of things were what they ought to be.
But when she turns and looks up, distracted by the old-fashioned sound
Of a biplane's engine stalling out of sight, she thinks she reads the fading
Signature of God etched backward in Art Deco gold leaf
Against the nosemarked storefront of the planet.

Someone is skywriting there, but she can't make out
What she has every right to believe is hers, something about love
And the world's being made and remade in the shape of her desire—
The content of rhetoric being purity, she being one of the chosen.

MECHANICS

Now I begin again to refuse to say the things
    I have refused to say all along:
How trucks on the turnpike raise a seizure
    of passage, a spasm in the plywood walls
Of this room where we lie in refugee heaps,
    too many for the pair of ruptured beds;
How venetian blinds slant radiance down on us
    like sea-illumination falling on certain fish
That mate only in this precise incidence of light.
    One of us is a father: a crowbar
Of neon touches his sleeping face;
    his peace is the stillness
Of the crushed after the bonemill lifts
    its powdery wheel. One of us is a mother:
She lies on her side between him and the wall,
    awake, expecting the shift
Of the sprocket. Many of us are scattered
    bodies of children, some ratcheted
On the second bed, some on the floor:
    dreamers less made of flesh
Than of one anothers' names, driven to this
    bedroom stained with the rainbow
Of factory oil and the darkness that beats
    at the world from inside the lower
Chambers of the heart of Christ. Hours
    from checkout time, the sleeping man
Makes an anonymous sound, a perfect glottal
    echo of 1957, martinis, Edsels on the freeway,

Eisenhower's golf swing, yellow Formica, the residue
   of Korean mortars showering down in the cheap-
Motelroom-cover of night. One child on the floor
   wakes up. His mother took him sleeping
From the backseat of the whipped-out Chevy,
   undressed him, laid him down. Now
He finds himself wearing only his faded
   underwear, and he shivers and whines
For the first time with his own peculiar shame
   at the thought of his naked skin. The mother
Stares at the window as if she could see
   a world beyond the chemical light that leaks
Through the blind-slats. She slips out of bed
   and covers her crying son with a sweater.
Something moves in the mirror's half-darkness.
   The shape she sees there could be anyone's,
Living or dead. She thinks she does not care
   what the dead are doing. She knows the dead
Do nothing, exactly like the rest of us.
   They are all on their way somewhere else.
None of them have jobs. This is the only transfiguration
   any of us here can understand: Three days and nights
And the money will be gone. By morning already
   light will come down harder, scarring us
With unconscious brilliance, burning. But now
   the woman feels a tingling in her hands
Where she touched the shrapnel-
   gashed flesh of his belly years ago in the silence
Of a bedroom like this one, and started turning out
   poverty after poverty, each granting itself
The luxury of an *I*: Every stroke of the piston bearing
   body after laboring body in
To the emptiness we call a living.

Rodney Jones

CARPE DIEM

Though pretty, it rarely worked, lining seduction
with worms or being always right, like some ideal
marvel of professors, when there was time for music,
which was never words so much as time. And the subject
of those songs we prayed all adolescence to become
was not love, really, but the loneliness love betrays:
summers immersed in childhood's various waters,
warm and cool springs weaving the plaid of Brushy Lake,
and letting it all go, that guilty underwater rush.
Such easy idylls as the ice cream truck interrupts
are what we have of abandon, though we would not leave.
Even while we were there, we were begging to return,
and some of the bodies springing from bumpered posts
had already grown breasts, strange hairs at the groin
like cursive signatures we had once itched to sign.
To speak of the body is to return to that very place
where the body was most alive, not to the corpse.
Those who think of bodies most haven't seen one,
not yet. While they endure the first hormonal surge,
their bodies answer even dreams with awkward thrusts
that seem to catch them in machines and hurt memory.
And they still harbor toys: stuffed animals forgetting
their names, incomplete sets, trucks with broken grilles.
Only their guarded silences seem unseasonably adult,
though each door stonewalls the moment of flesh

until the chrysalis breaks and they fall to each other.
In lachrymose spasms. In ripe seizures of abstract joy.
Still, I don't remember what hurt me most, the blue
and womanly corpse or the slim body of my first girl.
Perhaps because the corpse was family, in my mind
it seemed to surprise some shameful act of bestial love
that stuck the eyes on open. As for the girl,
since she lay in a half-dark backseat and cringed
a little out of childish modesty, I cannot swear I saw
the breasts embarking, the slow gift of the thighs,
but staggered afterwards from the car and sat a good
twenty minutes on a rock, drunk on nothing but sense
and alien fortune. I saw us married and quarrelsome
in a trailer beside the silo on her family's dairy farm,
and then, faintly, the edge of a harder embrace,
skull against cheek, ribcage against breast. The sky
wore that raincloud look of a poorly rinsed wound.
Both times attach me to a third and ring like a chord.
I grieved them both and loved steadily as I grieved,
but why do they come together now, corpse and girl?
—admonishing me, *Be quick and gentle as you change
seat to bed, sheet to shroud,* as though I were not
already all here and late maybe for the time of my life.

FAILED MEMORY EXERCISE

The water tank above the trees, and then the town,
Lord God, the sudden, blunt, exhilarating shock
Of pavement against the chert of the bottom road,

Bare schoolyard, white clinic, a block of stores
Like a test for names, beginning with the P.O.,
By which, in late autumn, the loaded wagons came,

The colts wheeling behind the great sober mares,
And turned east, clattering toward the cotton gin,
And returned empty, and faded beyond the tracks,

Beyond those yards, where one day the sallow
Dozers rolled and skinned back the flowerbeds
For the pumps and grease rack of the new Shell;

But begin again, for the dark green Lincoln rises
To its lube and crests where Zetty's kitchen was:
The black gush withers and dribbles to a drip,

And memory gums like shavings in the burnt oil
Now that plywood masks the windows of the stores,
Which test me as I bump awake above the Atlantic

Or wait in the plant-hung lobby of a hotel
In Atlanta or Montreal and answer then, though
I do not know the nature of the questions, true

Or false, fill-in-the-blanks south from the P.O.:
Three grocers, Leona Patterson's Fabric Box,
The shuttered bank, the poolhall din and smoke,

And this would have been a Saturday, *Sabrina*
Playing at the Cameo, the farmers scooping
Sweet feed and calf manna from the silvery bins

Of H. R. Summerford and Sons, General Merchandise,
But stop now, for I see the man without a nose
Like a pencil point ground to a nub and breaking

There against the efflorescence of the barbershop,
And stare again into that hole beneath the eyes
Where I must have thought I'd spy the brain itself

Before my gaze dropped to seize on missing tiles,
A blond curl, a plate engraved ACME MFG., INC.—
Those things that wore away and primed a vacancy.

But he sat there while my distant cousin shined his shoes,
And then he simply walked across Main to the depot,
A place I can't forget, since its beams were ripped out,

Numbered, and shipped east to some resurrection bistro
Where one can cop a decent blintz and espresso now
That the trains don't stop and no one's keeping store.

Yusef Komunyakaa

YELLOW DOG CAFÉ

In a cerulean ruckus
Of quilts, we played house
Off the big room where
They laughed & slowdragged
Weekends. *The eagle flies*
On Friday. The jukebox pulsed
A rainbow through papery walls.
We were paid a dollar to guard
Each other. I was eight
& S. C. Mae fourteen,
As we experimented with
The devil. Mill workers
Changed money in the briny
Glow of bootleg, overpowered
By the smell of collards, catfish,
& candied yams. Granddaddy Gabriel
Worked the cash register
Beside his second wife, Rosie
Belle. I heard my mother
& father laugh like swimmers
Underwater. A raw odor
Of lilies & sweat filled the room;
My cousin's hands moved over me
Smooth & tough as a blues guitar.
Somebody swore they saw

A silhouette with a gasoline can
The night S. C. Mae ran away
With a woman's husband.
For weeks they sifted ashes
But the gutted studs & braces
Only leaned against the wind,
Weak as a boy & girl entwined
On the floor. That June
Granddaddy drove a busload
Up north: the growers paid him
A dollar a day for each pair of hands.
He wanted to rebuild those nights,
Their circle of blurred cards.
The bus grunted between orchards,
& by late August I had enough
Fire-blackened nickels & dimes
To fill a sock, but only a few pickers
Came back after a season of wine-stained
Greenbacks sewn inside coats
& taped to the soles of their feet.

LOOKING FOR CHOCTAW

We put down our popguns
& cap pistols, & raised our hands
Into the air, hoping he'd step
From winterberry & hollyhock.
We flung ourselves in a circle
At sunset & fell in the dust,
But we couldn't trick him
Out. He'd walk in our footprints
When we were alone in the woods
Fishing or tracking a jackrabbit
Through wild-gray tobacco.
Heat figures waltzed to a killdeer

As we searched hollowed trees.
He remained in his unblinking
Stillness, years after toy guns
Became real ones tucked into belts.
When we parked with girlfriends
In our souped-up four-on-the-floor
Beside Mitch Creek & listened
To Fats Domino & The Shirelles
On WWEZ, we dared him to fight,
But he only left his breath
On windshields, as if nothing
Could hold him in this world.
Not even the fleshy hunger
Forged by what pulls
Greenness through a leaf.
Perhaps we betrayed mystery
So we could become shadows
Of dreamers, as fingers untangled
Saw vines & left us lost
To ourselves. Mama Mary
Was baking molasses tea cakes
Or stirring sugar into lemonade,
Deep in thought, when she turned
& I saw his face carved
Into hers.

GRISTMILL

Black hands shucked
& shelled corn into a washtub
While a circle of ancient voices
Hummed "Li'l Liza Jane."
Daddy shouldered a hundred-pound sack
To Mister Adam's gristmill.
The place was a moment of

Inertia. A horde of rough shoes
Against a revolving dancefloor.
Navel to navel. Slip-
Socket to ball-
Bearing & cogwheel.
Gears dragged & caught,
& the machine's calibrated
Rhythm kicked in.
An orgasm of golden dust
Clung to the wooden floor,
To the grass & leaves
Outside. A field holler
Travelled out, coming back
With the same sweaty cries
Elvis stole from R&B,
Like a millstone worn
Bright. Smooth, white hands
Halved the meal & husk:
One for you, two for me.

KNIGHTS OF THE WHITE CAMELLIA
& DEACONS OF DEFENSE

They were in a big circle
Beside Mitch Creek, as it murmured
Like a murderer tossing in his sleep
Between a wife & daughter, demure
As Sartre's Respectable Prostitute
On a feathered bed in July.
The sacrament. A gallon
Jug of bootleg passed from hand
To hand. An orgy of nightbirds
Screeched under the guillotined
Moon that hung like a target
Reflected against each robe.

Bibles, icons, & old lies. Names
Dead in their mouths like broken
Treaties. A spired & cupolaed
Dominion for bloodhounds. Apparitions
Tied to the Lily-cross & Curse.

Next day, in the hard light,
In a show of force,
Dark roses outbloomed
Camellias, a radiance
Not borrowed from the gleam
Of gun barrels. Sons
& daughters of sharecroppers
Who made sawmills
& cotton fields hum for generations,
Encircled the slow-footed
Marchers like an ebony shield.
Bullhorns blared, German
Shepherds whined on choke chains,
& swaggering clubs throttled spring.
Resistance startled crepe myrtle
& magnolia, while a clandestine
Perfume diluted the tear gas.

VILLON/LEADBELLY

Two bad actors canonized by ballads
flowering into dusk, crowned with hoarfrost.
But the final blows weren't dealt in Meung-
sur-Loire or the Angola pen. "Irene,
Irene, I'll see you in my dreams."

Unmoved by the hangman's leer,
these two roughhouse bards ignored
his finger traveling down the list.

They followed every season's penniless
last will & testament. Their songs

bleed together years. A bridge,
more than a ledger of bones.
Ghosts under the skin in bedlam,
Princes of Fools, they prowled
syncopated nights of wolfbane

& gin mills of starlight
at The Golden Mortar & The Bucket
of Blood, double-daring men across
thresholds, living down the list,
strung out on immortality's rag.

WORK

I won't look at her.
My body's been one
Solid motion from sunrise,
Leaning into the lawnmower's
Roar through pine needles
& crabgrass. Tiger-colored
Bumblebees nudge pale blossoms
Till they sway like silent bells
Calling. But I won't look.
Her husband's outside Oxford,
Mississippi, bidding on miles
Of timber. I wonder if he's buying
Faulkner's ghost, if he might run
Into Colonel Sartoris
Along some dusty road.
Their teenage daughter & son sped off
An hour ago in a red Corvette
For the tennis courts,

& the cook, Roberta,
Only works a half day
Saturdays. This antebellum house
Looms behind oak & pine
Like a secret, as quail
Flash through branches.
I won't look at her. Nude
On a hammock among elephant ears
& ferns, a pitcher of lemonade
Sweating like our skin.
Afternoon burns on the pool
Till everything's blue,
Till I hear Johnny Mathis
Beside her like a whisper.
I work all the quick hooks
Of light, the same unbroken
Rhythm my father taught me
Years ago: *Always give*
A man a good day's labor.
I won't look. The engine
Pulls me like a dare.
Scent of honeysuckle
Sings black sap through mystery,
Taboo, law, creed, what kills
A fire that is its own heart
Burning open the mouth.
But I won't look
At the insinuation of buds
Tipped with cinnabar.
I'm here, as if I never left,
Stopped in this garden,
Drawn to some Lotus-eater. Pollen
Explodes, but I only smell
Gasoline & oil on my hands,
& can't say why there's this bed
Of crushed narcissus
As if gods wrestled here.

Robert Morgan

THE ROAD FROM ELMIRA

The road through Saluda Gap and down
the Winding Stairs was the one
he took with hams and walnuts, mink
and ginseng, every year in the wagon
to Augusta, the same road drovers
across the mountains from Kentucky
used, negotiating the steep
turns below Panther, tying back
their wheels with hickory withes
for the worst grades. Leaving before light
he passed two nights in the fields
avoiding taverns, and stations for
the drovers pushing hogs and cattle,
even turkeys, to the markets
in the low country. Rifle under
the seat he prayed not to be
overtaken or waylaid. A cousin
disappeared who'd been a mason
on the statehouse in Columbia,
coming home with six months' pay.
When grocers on the riverfront
bargained down too low or hard,
he peddled door to door. That was
his only chance for Christmas cash,
for coffee for the backporch mill,

for sugar, cloth, boots, rifle
cartridges. Any surplus would go
for dictionaries, books, a long
auger for drilling pump logs to lead
springwater into the yard.

In the battle near Petersburg
the instant a bullet almost nudged
his temple, he saw the sniper
on a chestnut bough and, deaf with fear,
shot quick as at a squirrel.
But never saw the Yankee fall
for smoke from cannon screened the field
and when it cleared he found the cold
muzzles staring him down with grapeshot.
That's when he prayed the hardest yet,
and promised not to fire on anyone
again. Rumors during Reconstruction
had him shouting to a friend, "Let's go."
Crawling to the woods they threw
their weapons in the brush and ran
with raised arms behind the lines.
He wintered in the prison sheds near
the river at Elmira where
three thousand Tarheels would die
of exposure, where guards called him "Johnny"
when they brought the corncob soup.
In the blizzards he trapped
rodents and birds for meat. A rat
brought four cents for a blanket.
It was the gospel singing and prayer
that warmed them through the new year.
Wrapped in rags the soldiers sang
Old Harp numbers by the Chemung.
His throat swelled with diphtheria once
and he couldn't swallow or pronounce
his name. April with the snow just

rancid carcasses and the slush
in ditches pecked by blowing rain,
they put the survivors on trains
for the long ride south through greening hills,
ruined towns. Let out at Greenville
he saw on the distant mountains
sarvis and redbud in bloom. On
the first of May he walked past
the wasted city toward foothill mist.
The Lindsays in Travelers Rest
gave him supper and their guest
bedroom. At home his boxer barked
all night, and they said Frank must be back,
though they hadn't heard in a year,
neither telegram nor letter.
Next day he climbed the wagon track
and walked into the yard ghostlike
at milking time, scaring everyone
under the full spring-planting moon.

MICA COUNTRY

Here in the poorest mine country
in the dust of Dog Day drought,
the road itself glitters and weeds
along the bank and meadow sparkle.

In the dust of Dog Day drought
dirt of fields and spoil heap sides
along the bank and meadow sparkle,
and mud in the stream, all gilded.

Dirt of fields and spoil heap sides
and manure piles show millions,

and mud in streams, all gilded
with little mirrors, like fish scales,

and manure piles show millions
where a farmer plows a milky way
of little mirrors, like fish scales,
and each mote and grain is brighter,

where a farmer plows a milky way,
than dew or facet or window,
and each mote and grain is brighter
to reflect in luminous soil

through dew or facet or window,
the glare of blinding poverty
reflected in the luminous soil
here in the poorest mine country.

JUTACULLA ROCK

Up in Jackson County they have
this soapstone in a field, scored all over
with hieroglyphics no one has solved.
Or maybe it's more picture writing,
the figures so rough and worn
they no longer represent. But
the markings are at least distinct
enough to tell they're made with hands
and not just thaw and wind and water.
Among the written characters of all creation
that big rock seems significant, but
like the written characters of all
creation is unintelligible without
a key to its whorls and wisps
of scripture that seem to shiver

in the rain on its face
like fresh-ink chromosomes
or voice-prints of quasars, there
in the washed-out cornfield. But what
could be more awesome than a message
ancient, untranslatable, true,
up where giants walked on the balds,
in text and context, history, word?

HORACE KEPHART

Outside the tent on the Little Fork
of the Sugar Fork of Hazel Creek
a man is writing. His table boards
on upended kegs, he drafts meticulously clear
paragraphs and weights the finished pages
with a shotgun shell. Squirrels rippling
in the trees above do not distract him.
The jug by a white pine is stopped with a cob.

Each sentence he scratches with economy
is payment on a vast unpayable obligation:
to his parents for the years of college, for
the special courses at Cornell, for his tenure
cataloguing Petrarch in Florence, for the girl,
his Laura, married in Ithaca and taken
west, for the librarian's post in St. Louis,
for the study of Finnish, for the unwritten
history of western exploration that
excused long camping holidays and nights
away from home and expensive rare editions,
for the weeks of drinking and sulk.

Lean as a mountaineer himself, galluses
swung at his sides, he scribbles to the young

his intensity of woodcraft, weapons, survival,
and of the hillmen his archaic friends and landlords,
makers of spirits. Even now one's loose
hog crashes through the brush into his camp
and knocks a tentline from its stob so
the canvas home sags at one corner on
his narrow cot, and breaks the clothesline.
As he jumps to shout and whack it back
into the undergrowth the unfinished sheet
from an early chapter of *Our Southern Highlanders*
peels off the desk and luffs like a wounded
dove out through scrub and leaves to the creek.

MAN AND MACHINE

Besides drinking and telling lies,
nothing interested my cousin Luther
like working with the tractor.
Astride that bright and smelly beast
he was a man inspired.
Revving and tearing the stubble
of early spring he cussed
the metal like a favorite mule,
parrying any stallout with the shift.
In too big a hurry to turn
at the end of a row he jammed
in a brake and spun around,
lowered the harrows
into the winter-bleached field
and blasted off for yon end.
Barely able to read, he took
dusters and bush hogs and diesel movements
apart with the skill of a surgeon,
hollering on the phone for parts
as far away as Charlotte or Atlanta.

Would stay on his ass at the filling station
or country store for weeks
while wife and kids and parents
picked in the heat the crops he'd
drive to market. Neither storm-threat
nor overripening could move him
to join their labor. Until time
for dusting with the homemade blower
mounted on a jeep. Or after the vines
were cut he'd windlass in the long wires.
Winters Luther lived only for his truck,
banging down the dirt road to Chestnut Springs
for booze and women. But that was just
occasional. Most days he'd brag at the store
about his pickup, or be trading for another
with even thicker tires, more horsepower
and chrome, a gunrack in the window.
At home he'd maybe tune a little,
oil the plates of the planter.
But off the machine he was just
another stocky hoojer, yelling
to make up for his lack of size
and self-esteem, adding fat and blood
pressure. Late February breaking time
transformed him. He leapt on the big
diesel and burned out its winter farts
all the way to the bottoms, whipping
the animal until it glowed, became
his legs and voice and shoulders.
To children and himself he tore up ground
like a centaur. Plowing with the lights on
all night in the river fields
he circled more times than any race driver,
shouting in the settling damp while
we slept hearing the distant fury.
And by morning the fields were new.

George Scarbrough

LETTER TO SPENCER

Today, brother, I am at home writing,
And the earth is a bright, dun mule biting
The arm of the heart and the heart's shoulder.
"Another farm and house and one year older,"
Is the way the entry flows out from my pen.
But the heart sets other marks and beats them in
Today when mind is clear and memory good,
And earth is a bright, dun mule biting a wood.
Lee married, Edith grown, are names of ages
Reminding me we grew by lonely stages
Of someone gone, expanding rooms, a voice
Marked in the stillness subsequent to noise.
We grew by brothers leaving and the girl.
And now when earth's bright whinnying lips curl
Over the heart, I am grown from last year's leaving
Into this man whose youth is past believing;
I have been old before, but never before so old.
Today, brother, there is little news to be told
Except the wheat is heavy and the corn is young,
And Reuben came crying in the morning that he was stung
And peeled his shirt back to the mark of a thorn.
Reuben is growing, slim and blond as corn.
Lowery is plowing and hasn't much to say,
Keeping his tall dark self in his tall dark way.
And the land is usual, wind and sun and trees:

Nothing, it seems, can alter any of these.
There is not much to tell. Father and mother would
Send you their love and bid you to be good.
Walk quietly in strange towns, is my advice
Again, although you have resented twice
Before such words from a brother, especially
One who has yet his second town to see.
Give me an answer when you have time to spare
And tell me how the earth turns for you there.

CUTTING SOD-LAND

Under the bright disc the frog's blood was much brighter,
In sod-land rested five years, farmed in one.
I must confess my heart was something lighter
Before the harrow brought the frog's blood gleaming in the sun.

Bright as a scarlet flower sudden to the eye,
I must confess the blood leaped from the furrow,
Dazzled the clod with light caught from the sky
Mingled with light turned from the black-dark burrow.

Even the burrow itself showed its intense surprise
To find in its shallow room the harbor of such color.
Even as I turned down my sickened eyes,
Steadied the quaking heart, the ground at my feet was duller

Than sunlit field had ever shown before
With something wild and puzzled, something pale,
With finding out of that bright drip and pour.
I must confess now, now I must not fail

To make a full confession. Bright was the harrow's power,
Bright were the twelve discs driving, pulling in the sun:
Polished and bright as a white flint quarry tower,
In sod-land rested five years, farmed in one.

Yet bright as the disc, the frog's blood was much brighter:
Spilled on the earth, undarkened by the ground,
It cried to my heart, it wept for an hour much lighter,
It called for the wind and sun with an endless scarlet sound.

EASTWARD IN EASTANALLE

This is the heart's world. This is the land
Of the spirit, not the man-kept land
Of people and people's voices, but the land
Of clear blue mountains and cedar-colored skies;
Of green corn waving, of loneliness
Cool and separate in the waving corn.
This is the land of clouds as white as skulls
Or gelded flowers in the old valley, pale
As astonished moonflowers in the valley day.
This is the land of cool colors,
Of crystal, white and blue, and the tone of water
Welling from the low earth, the shallow white
And deep cedar of the running water
Colored over the earth. This is the tender land,
The indiscriminate land, green as corn,
Ripe as plums, that makes no choice among
Its people. All who are here, are here
And are the children. It makes no compromise,
Deals impartially in indistinctions,
And is kind and open to interpretations
Various as men who love it.

And to me
This is the heart's world, too lovely for bearing,
And marvelously crystal, cedar-colored, white
As white birds flying in the morning sun!
World of the lost heart on the edge of finding!
World of the unknown manner of men!

THE STORM

"You will not always have me here to say,
'The ghost is come!'" you said shortly.
And white lightning past the second point
Browsed through your words with exclamatic fury,
Much too strong for the occasion and the time
And the quiet tenure of your tongue.

The slim well of the cliff
Was spitting the wind out of its wretched teeth.
Between an earth of lovers, these are the choicest words.
Say them, and they are said.
No one will break his mind on them,
No one in my household.

But over the valley there seemed surprise,
As if they watched, the dread illiterate houses,
The face of the rock and the misbehavior of God.
Under the white stress of lightning, feeling the stunned
Episode of passion work in guesses,
And the crippled craze grow savagely conjectural,

Darkly discreet, who leaned out of what window?
No, I cannot affirm that the land was real,
That there was a valley with its certain texture,
Or vouch for the soft lucidity of stone.
Nor can, I think, you, lecturing me there
With the civil absolution of your tongue.

The rain glanced on the second point, cold and charming;
And the well of the cliff spat out the cloudy
Climb of the wind.
It is not easy to remember pity and the ways of possessing,
Or possessing and the ways of pity.

FIELD BEYOND THE RIDGE

Beyond the ridge there is a field of grass
And a place for sleeping on the sunny ground.
It is a high field, leaning in the wind,
Bare of field-sight, disturbed by high ridge-sound

No more than ears stopped up by heavy acres
Of yellow herd's grass ever understand.
I love to lie there in the withes of summer
And pour the spotted seed from hand to hand,

Before I drop to sleep. A yellow leaf,
Turning from ridges like a weight-warped wheel
Above the yellow ground, is how sleep comes
To that ridge-hidden, sun-influenced field.

Cool seed against the hollow of the throat
Is how sleep comes to that high world of dun
And windy acres, bridging valley-width,
From ridge to ridge, in that slow valley sun.

I love to lie there with the sound of water
Where water never was, above the lower
Spring half a mile away, inside a field
That halts a creek and stops a valley floor,

And sleep an autumn sleep in seeded hay
That stood beyond the need of hook and blade,
Losing my five-foot-seven length for good
In slanting acres of that yellow shade.

Beyond the ridge there is a field of grass
Yellow as sun, and a creek gone underground.
It is a high field, leaning in the wind;
It is a field my knowing heart has found.

HYMN FOR THE SOUND OF HYMNS

After the deaths I've seen in Eastanalle Valley,
On the points of earth the bitter hymn
Purloined by wind whose route is not by heaven,
And on the grass the horizontal prayer
Caught like the dried seeds in the tough purple web,
I am immune, I do not deal in qualms.

This is no time for female mind-orgasms.
Weeping is out of style, like the old hats
Women wear to the ungodly numerous funerals;
Though like old hats, there are those who wear it,
Knowing nothing better, or liking
The conservative feeling that sometimes stirs a crowd.

A man can have enough of anything;
Even the voluntary venture of the grave-diggers' league
Grows a trifle less ideal with increased business.
The sod is as tough as hell in Eastanalle Valley
Under the purple grass.

Here is where the stone
Rolls over the vulnerable belly and smells the ground
With sure proof of man's unsweet divinity:
Is gorgeous insult to those who must do the work
Of cleaning up and filling the hole in after.

To me it is immoral to die in such fashion.
Just as it was immoral for Bruce, my friend,
To die seven years and stink before he finished,
Stuck to the bed, and to be buried
With the filthy sheet cut to fit his size.
Or Lake Winters, worked to a walking corpse
In the fields of another man, to fall exhausted,
With the heart steamed out of his pitiful body.
There was no dignity
The day they went to their burial.

Weeping is out of style, like the old hats
Women wear to the ungodly numerous funerals,
Because they are all they have, or because
They are not wise to late dictates of fashion.
Weeping is ante-twenty, ante-bellum, ante-diluvian.
Weeping is not for the smothered face, the mouth's
Bewildered sneering. Weeping is not for dignity.

Anger is weeping now, fury is muscle's spasm,
After the deaths I've seen in Eastanalle Valley.
On the points of earth the bitter hymn
Purloined by wind whose route is not by heaven,
And on the grass the horizontal prayer
Caught short like dried seeds in the tough purple web,
Make me immune, make me twice dead to qualms.

Dave Smith

NEW ORLEANS ENGAGEMENT

First shivers of palm fronds lift over the French Quarter.
Hurricane's coming through courtyards, alleys,
beating the pompon clusters of oak leaves to convulse
then wheeze and catch a breath. Pieces of grit,
green, gold, swirl up at the eye, sparkly as Mardi Gras
gifts flung against doors, and now clouds
blackpile and whisk by, as if all's changed, the world's
putting on the blue of evening, a sickly green
wads the laketop, and the sky's got yellow veins. Here's
enough to make you see what fear is, all you
can do about it, too, so I swing with a grip on a tumbler
of Jameson, sweeping my watch where
a fence-top swears beauty won't last, flowers fly apart.
I'd like to have eyes that don't miss a thing
but I'll settle for bigger shapes, the feeling a storm brings
as it gains weight, like love, shoving, thrashing
Ponchartrain's placid waters to froth and lap, neither salt
nor whatever's not. This marsh stays dangerous.
As any big breather knows, life's a shallow
bowl, so I want to know what's what, get my boat
where my fingers don't have to dig in deep wood. You can
see what people's faces look like once the spray
spreads its egg-white all over, you can say what warmish
sluices sag in their underwear. The days I love
break and bring me to see you cooking red beans, rice,

maybe cornbread, too, hair all wispy, sound
of wind and things falling what I hear, so I make my song.
I catch you coming, barefooted, to the door,
worry's music faint, in the skin of your dress, and I think
how those in the boats are thinking this is the last
of everything, last trip away from the house, last redfish,
last memory of good luck, last chance to say
Please, God, I love her or that *Please* that doesn't know
the end of its thought. Like me, when I see
you pouring the Bordeaux, who called and asked me to come
home for the storm that wants us to eat alone,
or not at all, and is shaking the trees like a voodoo spirit
saying not here, not now, maybe not tomorrow.

THE LOUISIANA SEA OF FAITH

This land lies low toward the Gulf, a ridge
halved by the Mississippi, abandoned
where great sturgeon, shark, turtles loomed,
our daily rising mist the last letting go,
breath's rot fertile enough to root the lush
cycling of the short-lived and the hopeless.
Twice annually our people cry out and binge
for lives drained in the torque of a death
that clings like sodden summer shirts: Mardi Gras,
Christmas balance priests and bare-breasted women.
The winter sun yanks orchids from the darkness.
Men drift past the levee like beer cans, our mothers,
our daughters rasp "Throw me something, Mister."

NIGHT TRAFFIC NEAR WINCHESTER,
VIRGINIA

From Cumberland's funerals, eldest son, I
lead my survivors south, toward the sea,

past tall ash, through stunning cidery
winesaps still bobbing the Blue Ridge,
the leaf-littered fieldstone walls
drooping like rebel stragglers away
from weathered barns, veterans leaning
quaint as postcards from the dark
Tomb of the Confederate Dead, never
closed, catching the trucks' roar
at Winchester where my father always
stopped to eat. Here, we descend

into the Valley, slow to a stop-and-go,
crawl through painted brick cottages
huddled at sidewalks like history,
heartpine floors sloped so badly
water runs off before it stains.
Like the hips of ancestors, each
foundation is cracked and patched,
the windows narrow as eyes, crusty
along the once horse-clotted street.
Tourists find here the cheery, yellow
farmhouse used by Stonewall Jackson
to plot cavalry raids thunderous
as the black Bible he slept with.
It's dark as a mapcase now, closed.

I promise kids we'll stop another time,
long enough to see boots, old orders,
the grim portraits staring at war,
but now we climb, car straining, up
the dark's deadly ridge, and halt
before our drop to the plains. Here
my father stopped with me, heading
north to bury the fallen kin. Stepping
out, I feel the chill, rare night drift
me back to the smell of his coffee.

This is the way to grandmother's, he'd say,
pointing into the sky, so I say it,
on the cliff, no grandmother left, and
behind us nothing's changed, motors
howl all night, voices that roar
as teamsters did, hearing the rumor—
"Grant's taken Charlottesville,"
but tonight just the march of boys
looking for girls, trucks for home.
It's only Route 17, the country way.

But my son, old as I was with my father,
climbs over our girls sleeping, steps
to the overlook's lipfall I don't
need to look at, the historical blank
that never stops falling here. Still,
I come behind him, take his hand.
His athletic jacket shines like cities
at Christmas, its faint galaxies
of light shifting as the body moves.
Out there we see the neon welcome
of blue Sears, Kmart red, streets
steady with taillights like campfires.

When once I asked my father which army
was here those long nights, he said
We were men, just going up and down.
Afraid, he said, glad for a fire.
Our fathers and fathers of fathers.
In the cold of mountains I'm afraid
at this edge and feel the hand asking
"How far have we come?" I could say
I don't know, the usual evasion,
but over the lights, the dotted road,
I hear an old voice I had thought lost
say *Far, but not far enough yet.*
Ahead, our family will stand awake,
lights on, coffee hot, ready for news.

CUMBERLAND STATION

Gray brick, ash, hand-bent railings, steps so big
it takes hours to mount them, polished oak
pews holding slim hafts of sun, and one
splash of the *Pittsburgh Post-Gazette*. The man
who left Cumberland gone, come back, no job
anywhere. I come here alone, shaken
the way I came years ago to ride down
mountains in Big Daddy's cab. He was
the first set cold in the black meadow.

Six rows of track, photographed, gleam, rippling
like water on walls where famous engineers steam, half
submerged in frothing crowds with something
to celebrate and plenty to eat. One's mine,
taking children for a free ride, a frolic
like an earthquake. Ash cakes his hair.
I am one of those who walked uphill
through flowers of soot to zing
scared to death into the world.

Now whole families afoot cruise South Cumberland
for something to do, no jobs, no money for bars,
the old stories cracked like wallets.

This time there's no fun in coming back. The second
death. My roundhouse uncle coughed his youth
into a gutter. His son slid on the ice,
losing his need to drink himself
stupidly dead. In this vaulted hall
I think of all the dirt poured down
from shovels and trains and empty pockets.
I stare into the huge malignant headlamps
circling the gray walls and catch a stuttered
glimpse of faces stunned like deer on a track.

Churning through the inner space of this godforsaken
wayside, I feel the ground try to upchuck and I dig

my fingers in my temples to bury a child
diced on a cowcatcher, a woman smelling
alkaline from washing out the soot.
Where I stood in that hopeless, hateful room
will not leave me. The scarf of smoke I saw
over a man's shoulder runs through me
like the sored Potomac River.

Grandfather, you ask why I don't visit you
now you have escaped the ticket-seller's cage
to fumble hooks and clean the Shakespeare reels.
What could we catch? I've been sitting in the pews
thinking about us a long time, long enough to see
a man can't live in jobless, friendless Cumberland
anymore. The soot owns even the fish.

I keep promising I'll come back, we'll get out,
you and me, like brothers, and I mean it.
A while ago a man with the look of a demented cousin
shuffled across this skittery floor and snatched up
the *Post-Gazette* and stuffed it in his coat
and nobody gave a damn because nobody cares
who comes or goes here or even who steals
what nobody wants: old news, photographs
of dead diesels behind chipped glass.

I'm the man who stole it and I wish you were here
to beat the hell out of me because what you said
a long time ago welts my face and won't go away.
I admit it isn't mine, even if it's nobody's.
Anyway, that's all I catch today—bad news.
I can't catch my nephew's life, my uncle's,
Big Daddy's, yours, or the ash-haired kids'
who fell down to sleep here after the war.

Outside new families pick their way along tracks
you and I have walked home on many nights.

Every face on the walls goes on smiling,
and, Grandfather, I wish I had the guts
to tell you this is a place I hope
I never have to go through again.

ON A FIELD TRIP AT FREDERICKSBURG

The big steel tourist shield says maybe
fifteen thousand got it here. No word
of either Whitman or one uncle
I barely remember in the smoke
that filled his tiny mountain house.

If each finger were a thousand of them
I could clap my hands and be dead
up to my wrists. It was quick
though not so fast as we can do it
now, one bomb, atomic or worse,
the tiny pod slung on wingtip,
high up, an egg cradled
by some rapacious mockingbird.

Hiroshima canned nine times their number
in a flash. Few had the time
to moan or feel the feeling
ooze back in the groin.

In a ditch I stand
above Mayre's Heights, the bookish
faces of Brady's fifteen-year-old
drummers, before battle, rigid
as August's dandelions
all the way to the Potomac
rolling in my skull.

If Audubon came here, the names
of birds would gush, the marvel
single feathers make
evoke a cloud, a nation,
a gray blur preserved
on a blue horizon, but
there is only a wandering child,
one dark stalk snapped off
in her hand. Hopeless teacher,
I take it, try to help her
hold its obscure syllables
one instant in her mouth,
like a drift of wind
at the forehead, the front door,
the black, numb fingernails.

Henry Taylor

AT SOUTH FORK CEMETERY

It had no voice, or anything like that,
as it came across a field to where we stood
cleaning up an overgrown burial ground—
a quiet whirlwind we could see was there
by leaves it spiraled higher than the trees.

It slapped a leaf or two against our bodies,
then wandered on across the empty road.
As if the thoughtless world were generous,
we took that quirk of air as something given,
and turned to cutting brush and righting stones.

A BARGAIN AT HALF THE PRICE

for Steve Canty

On a blasted heath in Maryland
There stands a livestock auction house
Where, every other Wednesday, men come
From miles around to buy and sell
Cheap saddles, swap lies and horses.
One night, I remember, they
Auctioned off one hundred plastic
Crucifixes, one at a time.

Riders in cowboy boots and red
T-shirts take the horses
Up the aisle and back, while
The auctioneer, known as Honest John,
Pries loose the bids and shouts them out.
"Sixty dollars! God damn it,
Gentlemen, let us pray!"
In the stands men drink big
Orange drinks and sit with girls
In tight blue slacks, with dyed black hair.

Once a month, from somewhere comes
A little man with a big trunk.
He stands in the center of the ring
And pulls out halters, buckets,
Reins, a saddle with one stirrup
("Here, gentlemen, we have a saddle
For a one-legged man!"), until
You think he has some magic power.

Someone has said that once a man
Walks through the doors of X's
Livestock Market, he is forever
Doomed. He may be right. I like
To think that while he stands
Beneath that roof, it is sanctuary,
And for anything he says or does
God has forgiven him already.

GOODBYE TO THE OLD FRIENDS

Because of a promise I cannot break
I have returned to my father's house, and here,
for the first time in years, I have risen
early this Sunday to visit the Friends.

As I drive to the Meeting House, the trees
wave softly as the wind moves over me.

I am late. Faces turn to look at me;
I sit in a pew apart, and silence breaks
slightly, like the rustle of old trees.
I wonder whether I am welcome here,
but in the old wall clock I see a friend.
An old man I remember now has risen

to say that this is Easter. Christ has risen.
The ticking of the old wall clock distracts me
as this old man addresses his friends;
he prowls for an hour through a Bible, breaks
his voice to bring my wandering mind back here
from aimless circling through the aging trees

whose branches tick like clocks. Boughs cut from trees,
disposed through the room, remind me of the risen
Christ this voice speaks of; I do not see him here.
I do not see him here, but flowers tell me,
on the mantel before us, in scent that breaks
above the graying heads of nodding Friends,

on hats and in lapels of aging Friends,
the flowers and the branches from the trees
remind me of what this old man's voice breaks
for the last time to tell us: Christ has risen.
With the tongue of a man he speaks to me
and to his Friends: there are no angels here.

At last I shout without breath my first prayer here
and ask for nothing but silence. Two old Friends
turn slowly toward each other, letting me
know how much silence remains. The trees
ripple the silence, and the spirit has risen.
Two old hands of marble meet and Meeting breaks.

Old Friends move over the lawn, among old trees.
One offers me his hand. I have risen,
I am thinking, as I break away from here.

THE HUGHESVILLE SCYTHE

The hills where I grew up had learned to hide
destructions from each other long before
Hughesville saw destruction take its store,
and still the Hughesville legend has not died:

how once the storekeeper unlocked the door
to find he had been robbed. One clue, beside
the hearth, a swallow's nest on the stone floor,
told him how the burglar had got inside.

The old man took a scythe-blade from his store
and fixed it in the chimney, across the fine-
edged dark, where it would split a man who tried
to come that way again and steal his gold.

No burglar ever came. Now those designs
are choked in honeysuckle, and the old
insistent rituals of decay unfold:
yet in my brain that unused blade still shines,

and when I try to walk through dark I hold
my hand before me, touching solid signs,
thinking how a man can hunt for gold
and lie in pieces in the raging vines.

BUILDINGS AND GROUNDS
for Richard Dillard

The house we moved into has been landscaped
    so that it has the portable, plastic look
    of a Sears, Roebuck toy farm.

All up and down our street, the same minor artist seems
  to have been at work; our neighbors' lawns are
  watered and mowed truly until they are carpets,

their shrubs are lovingly trimmed and shaped
  into green velvet eggs and spheres.
  Our neighbors watch us like hawks,

wondering whether we have the equipment,
  the know-how, the spirit, to strive with them
  as they strive with their landscapes.

Oh, let me bring my home from the South to this street!
  I will let the grass grow until it is knee-high,

I will import chickens and a blue-tick hound to trample
  the grass and dig bone-holes and scratch-holes,

I will set up on cinderblocks in the front yard
  a '38 Ford with no tires or headlights,

I will sit in the gutted driver's seat
  with a bottle of Old Mr. Mac, glaring at my
  neighbors, reading aloud from *God's Little Acre,*

I will be a prophet of wildness and sloth!

But the Puritan gaze of my neighbors cuts through
  my desperate vision of home—my dream house
  will not flourish here.

I will spend my rapidly declining years
  reading the labels on bags of crabgrass killer,

pushing my lawn mower until my front yard
  is as smooth as a green on a golf course,

clipping and shaping my landlord's opulent shrubs.

But don't misunderstand me—I have not been
   converted; I will still make something
   to sustain me here in this alien land.

I will plant mint in the flowerbeds beside
   the Shasta daisies we brought from Monticello,

I will set up a croquet course on the front lawn
   with a slender drink-stand at each wicket
   to hold my frosty mint juleps,

I will station an iron jockey by the driveway
   to stare back into the pitiless eyes
   of my neighbors' pink plastic flamingoes,

I will keep a Tennessee Walking Horse in the garage
   and give him a foxhound for company,

I will stand out front in a white linen suit
   surveying my plantation,

I will plant a magnolia tree.

But now, at the height of my visionary ecstasy,
   the telephone rings. It is the man
   next door, calling to let me know

that my sprinkler is turned up too high
   and is sprinkling the seats of his convertible.

I go out to turn down the water, and I see
   that the cedar needs trimming again,
   that the elm twigs need to be raked.

I will do those things. I will hoe and trench
   and weed, I will mow the grass.
   I have moved in here now,

and I have to do what I can.

Ellen Bryant Voigt

VISITING THE GRAVES

All day we travel from bed to bed, our children
clutching homemade bouquets
of tulips and jonquils, hyacinth,
handfuls of yellow salad from the fields.
In Pittsylvania County our dead face east,
my great-grandfather and his sons facing
what is now a stranger's farm.
One great-uncle chose a separate hill,
an absence in the only photograph.
Under the big oak, we fumble for his name
and the names of sisters scattered like coins.
But here is my father, near the stone
we watched him weep beside for twenty years.
And my mother beside him, the greenest slab of grass.
By horse, it was hours to Franklin County,
to Liberty Christian Church where her mother lies.
The children squabble in the car, roll on the velvet
slope of the churchyard, pout or laugh as we point out
the gap in the mountain where *her* mother's grave
is underwater, the lake lapping the house, the house
still standing like a tooth. We tell them how
we picked huckleberries from the yard,
tell them what a huckleberry is, but the oldest
can't keep straight who's still alive, the smallest
wants her flowers back—who can blame them,

this far from home, tired of trying
to climb a tree of bones. They fall asleep
halfway down the road, and we fall silent, too,
who were taught to remember and return,
my sister is driving, I'm in the back,
the sky before us a broken field of cloud.

STONE POND

Driving over the limit
on a mountain road,
the mist rising, Stone Pond
white with ice and white mist
inside its circle
of birch and black fir:

driving home after
seeing friends, the radio
complicitous and loud,
Beethoven's braided musical line,
a sonata I recall
playing well:

passing the tiny houses
on the hillside, woodsmoke
rising among the budded trees,
then passing within inches
of someone's yard: I circle
Stone Pond, and despair

seems like something I can set aside.
The road bends again, the morning
burns through the mist.
Sufficient joy—
what should I have done to make it last?

AT THE MOVIE: VIRGINIA, 1956

This is how it was:
they had their own churches, their own schools,
schoolbuses, football teams, bands and majorettes,
separate restaurants, in all the public places
their own bathrooms, at the doctor's
their own waiting room, in the *Tribune*
a column for their news, in the village
a neighborhood called Sugar Hill,
uneven rows of unresponsive houses
that took the maids back in each afternoon—
in our homes used the designated door,
on Trailways sat in the back, and at the movie
paid at a separate entrance, stayed upstairs.
Saturdays, a double feature drew the local kids
as the town bulged, families surfacing
for groceries, medicine and wine,
the black barber, white clerks in the stores—crowds
lined the sidewalks, swirled through the courthouse yard,
around the stone soldier and the flag,

and still I never *saw* them on the street.
It seemed a chivalric code
laced the milk: you'd try not to look
and they would try to be invisible.
Once, on my way to the creek,
I went without permission to the tenants'
log cabin near the barns, and when Aunt Susie
opened the door, a cave yawned, and beyond her square,
leonine, freckled face, in the hushed interior,
Joe White lumbered up from the table, six unfolding
feet of him, dark as a gun-barrel, his head bent
to clear the chinked rafters, and I caught
the terrifying smell of sweat and grease,
smell of the woodstove, nightjar, straw mattress—

This was rural Piedmont, upper south;
we lived on a farm but not in poverty.
When finally we got our own TV, the evening news
with its hooded figures of the Ku Klux Klan
seemed like another movie—*King Solomon's Mines,*
the serial of Atlantis in the sea.
By then I was thirteen,
and no longer went to movies to see movies.
The downstairs forged its attentions forward,
toward the lit horizon, but leaning a little
to one side or the other, arranging the pairs
that would own the county, stores and farms, everything
but easy passage out of there—
and through my wing-tipped glasses the balcony
took on a sullen glamor: whenever the film
sputtered on the reel, when the music died
and the lights came on, I swiveled my face
up to where they whooped and swore,
to the smoky blue haze and that tribe
of black and brown, licorice, coffee,
taffy, red oak, sweet tea—

wanting to look, not knowing how to see,
I thought it was a special privilege
to enter the side door, climb the stairs
and scan the even rows below—trained bears
in a pit, herded by the stringent rule,
while they were free, lounging above us,
their laughter pelting down on us like trash.

BLUE RIDGE

Up there on the mountain road, the fireworks
blistered and subsided, for once at eye level:

spatter of light like water flicked from the fingers;
the brief emergent pattern; and after the afterimage bled
from the night sky, a delayed and muffled thud
that must have seemed enormous down below,
the sound comcomitant with the arranged
threat of fire above the bleachers.
I stood as tall and straight as possible,
trying to compensate, trying not to lean in my friend's
direction. Beside me, correcting height, he slouched
his shoulders, knees locked, one leg stuck out
to form a defensive angle with the other.
Thus we were most approximate
and most removed.
                    In the long pauses
between explosions, he'd signal conversation
by nodding vaguely toward the ragged pines.
I said my children would have loved the show.
He said we were watching youth at a great distance,
and I thought how the young
are truly boring, unvaried as they are
by the deep scar of doubt, the constant afterimage
of regret—no major tension in their bodies, no tender
hesitation, they don't yet know
that this is so much work, scraping
from the self its multiple desires; don't yet know
fatigue with self, the hunger for obliteration
that wakes us in the night at the dead hour
and fuels good sex.
                    Of course I didn't say it.
I realized he watched the fireworks
with the cool attention he had turned on women
dancing in the bar, a blunt uninvested gaze
calibrating every moving part, thighs,
breasts, the muscles of abandon.
I had wanted that gaze on me.
And as the evening dwindled to its nub,

its puddle of tallow, appetite without object,
as the men peeled off to seek
the least encumbered consolation
and the women grew expansive with regard—
how I managed so long to stand among the paired
bodies, the raw pulsing music driving
loneliness into the air like scent,
and not be seized by longing,
not give anything to be summoned
into the larger soul two souls can make?
Watching the fireworks with my friend,
so little ease between us,
I see that I have armed myself;
fire changes everything it touches.

Perhaps he has foreseen this impediment.
Perhaps when he holds himself within himself,
a sheathed angular figure at my shoulder,
he means to be protective less of him
than me, keeping his complicating rage
inside his body. And what would it solve
if he took one hand from his pocket,
risking touch, risking invitation—
if he took my hand it would not alter
this explicit sadness.
      The evening stalls,
the fireworks grow boring at this remove.
The traffic prowling the highway at our backs,
the couples, the families scuffling on the bank
must think us strangers to each other. Or,
more likely, with the celebrated fireworks thrusting
their brilliant repeating designs above the ridge,
we simply blur into the foreground,
like the fireflies dragging among the trees
their separate, discontinuous lanterns.

THE SPRING

Beneath the fabric of leaves,
sycamore, beech, black oak,
in the slow residual movement
of the pool;
            in the current
braiding over the wedged branch,
and pouring from the ledge,
urgent, lyric,
            the source
marshalls every motion
to the geometric plunder of rock—
arranging a socket of water,
a cold estate
where the muscle wound
in the deep remission of light
waits
      for the white enamel dipper,
the last release, the rush,
the blunt completion

HOUSE

This orphaned house. Its needs, its presences.

Something brought us here—how else
could we, raw mourners,
have found it
tucked under the hill beside the sea?

Everything still stands
from previous lives: well, woodstove,
the feather tick imprinted
with so many bodies.

This place survives their multiple
amputations. The tug on the nipple
after the baby is gone,
after the breast is gone.

Trimming the wicks, setting the oak table—
when I move the air gives,
feels polished, I fill
the waiting sleeve with movement.

And everywhere the proprietary swallows.

      *   *   *

The body learns to incorporate its pain.
Sorrow lodged in the kitchen.
Stepsister. She-who-remembers. There,
in the corner, she worked her practical
arts—intaglio and salt-cure:

> A splash of brine on the table,
> hot iron, knife-slip, a scar,
> a trough, the table webs
> with stains and scratches.
> Deep into the water's
> grain, a boat engraves
> its habits. The wake
> has healed but retains
> the shape of the hull,
> the wound of the rudder.

   *   *   *

I have my routine.

The garden calls me to its harvesting.
The well needs me to draw up water.

From the seawind, I read tomorrow's
weather. The swallows surround us.

Evenings, we sit inside,
under the wing of the unfinished attic.

Here, in this place, this parentage,
we live with loss, a child's repeating absence.

HOLLY AND HICKORY

Rain, all night, taps the holly.
It ticks like a telegraph on the pane.
If awake in that house, meditating some old folly
Or trying to live an old pleasure again,
I could hear it sluicing the ruts in the land.

Rain beats down the last leaf of hickory,
But where I lie now rain sounds hint less
At benign sleight of the seasons, or Time's adept trickery,
And with years I feel less joy or distress
To hear water moving in wheel ruts, star-glintless,

And if any car comes now up that lane,
It carries nobody I could know,
And who wakes in that house now to hear the rain
May fall back to sleep—as I, long ago,
Who dreamed dawnward; and would rise to go.

THE WELL HOUSE

What happened there, it was not much,
But was enough. If you come back,
Not much may be *too much,* even if you have your old knack

Of stillness, and do not touch
A thing, a broken toy or rusted tool or any such
Object you happen to find
Hidden where, uncontrolled, grass and weeds bend.

The clematis that latches the door
Of the ruinous well house, you might break it.
Though guessing the water foul now, and not thirsting to take it,
With thirst from those years before
You might lean over the coping to stare at the water's dark-glinting floor.
Yes, that might be the event
To change *not much* to *too much,* and more than meant.

Yes, Truth is always in balance, and
Not much can become *too much* so quick.
Suppose you came back and found your heart suddenly sick,
And covered your sight with your hand:
Your tears might mean more than the thing you wept for but did not
                    understand.
Yes, something might happen there
If you came back—even if you just stood to stare.

IN MOONLIGHT, SOMEWHERE, THEY ARE SINGING

Under the maples at moonrise—
Moon whitening top leaf of the white oak
That rose from the dark mass of maples and range of eyes—
They were singing together, and I woke

From my sleep to the whiteness of moon-fire,
And deep from their dark maples, I
Could hear the two voices shake silver and free, and aspire
To be lost in moon-vastness of the sky.

My young aunt and her young husband
From their dark maples sang, and though

Too young to know what they meant I was happy and
So slept, for I knew I would come to know.

But what of the old man awake there,
As the voices, like vine, climbed up moonlight?
What thought did he think of past time as they twined bright in moon-air,
And veined, with their silver, the moon-flesh of night?

Far off, I recall, in the barn lot,
A mule stamped, once; but the song then
Was over, and for that night, or forever, would not
Resume—but should it again,

Years after, wake me to white moon-fire
On pillow, high oak leaf, and far field,
I should hope to find imaged in what new voices aspire
Some life-faith yet, by my years, unrepealed.

IN ITALIAN THEY CALL THE BIRD *CIVETTA*

The evening drooped toward owl-call,
The small moon slid pale down the sky,
Dark was decisive in cedars,
But dust down the lane dreamed pale,
And my feet stirred that dust there—
Ah, I see that Kentucky scene
Now only behind my shut eyelids,
As in this far land I stand
At the selfsame ambiguous hour
In the heart's ambiguity,
And Time is crumpled like paper
Crushed in my hand, while here
The thin moon slants pale down the pale sky,
And the small owl mourns from the moat.

This small owl calls from the moat now.
That other owl answers him
Across all the years and miles that
Are the only Truth I have learned,
And back from the present owl-call
Burns backward the blaze of day,
And the passage of years, like a tire's scream,
Fades now while the reply
Of a dew-damp and downy lost throat spills
To quaver from that home-dark,
And frame between owl-call and owl-call,
Life's bright parenthesis.

    The thin moon slants pale down the pale sky:
    The small owl mourns from the moat.

SITTING ON FARM LAWN ON SUNDAY AFTERNOON

The old, the young—they sit.
And the baby on its blanket

Blows a crystalline
Bubble to float, then burst

Into air's nothingness.
Under the maples they sit,

As the limpid year uncoils
With a motion like motionlessness,

While only a few maple leaves
Are crisping toward yellow

And not too much rust yet
Streaks the far blades of corn.

The big white bulldog dozes
In a patch of private shade.

The afternoon muses onward,
Past work, past week, past season,

Past all the years gone by,
And delicate feminine fingers,

Deft and ivory-white,
And fingers steely, or knobbed

In the gnarl of arthritis, conspire
To untangle the snarl of years

Which are their past, and the past
Of kin who in dark now hide,

Yet sometimes seem to stare forth
With critical, loving gaze,

Or deeper in darkness weep
At wisdom they learned too late.

Is all wisdom learned too late?
The baby lalls to itself,

For it does not yet know all
The tales and contortions of Time.

Nor do I, who sit here alone,
In another place, and hour.

WAS IT ONE OF THE LONG HUNTERS OF KENTUCKY WHO DISCOVERED BOONE AT SUNSET?

The seasons turn like a great wheel
Jogging on whimsies of weather, sometimes
Slipping backward a bit, or even about to heel
Over, paying no attention to chimes

Or clock-tick, seasons themselves being
The great clock to state our fate.
There are many small signs such as seeing
Boot heel-mark in wild mud, or toward the gate

And civilization, the grid in snow
Of overshoes, and smoke from the chimney, pale
Against twilight. There will come, you know,
A time for petunias, and loam black under thumbnail.

You feel a mystic reality
In loam's cool touch. But not long later you will lose
Yourself in the glimmering beech wood, high
On the mountain, above you nothing to choose

Between patches of summer sky's heavenly blue
Or green leaf's translucence against blue light,
And later those leaves will hang gold against blue,
And the heart swell to a new delight.

But you might as well remember that deer
In winter have starved before the first bud
Has offered frail sustenance, and the clear-
Eyed lynx forgets not the taste of blood.

Yes, in such ambiguity
The seasons wheel, and our hearts colder

Grow, under every kind of sky,
From early years to years that grow grimly older.

But I think how once in his long, lone wilderness walk
Across Kentucky—alone, sun low, arms crossed to prop his
Face up, they found Boone singing in his tuneless crow-squawk,
In joy just because the world is the way it is.

Charles Wright

HARDIN COUNTY
CPW, 1904–1972

There are birds that are parts of speech, bones
That are suns in the quick earth.
There are ice floes that die of cold.
There are rivers with many doors, and names
That pull their thread from their own skins.
Your grief was something like this.

Or self-pity, I might add, as you did
When you were afraid to sleep,
And not sleep, afraid to touch your bare palm;
Afraid of the wooden dog, the rose
Bleating beside your nightstand; afraid
Of the slur in the May wind.

It wasn't always like that, not in those first years
When the moon went on without its waters,
When the cores blew out of their graves in Hardin County.
How useless it is to cry out, to try
And track that light, now
Reduced to a grain of salt in the salt snow.

I want the dirt to go loose, the east wind
To pivot and fold like a string.
I want the pencil to eat its words,

The star to be sucked through its black hole.
And everything stays the same,
Locks unpicked, shavings unswept on the stone floor.

The grass reissues its green music; the leaves
Of the sassafras tree take it and pass it on;
The sunlight scatters its small change.
The dew falls, the birds smudge on their limbs.
And, over Oak Hill, the clouds, those mansions of nothingness,
Keep to their own appointments, and hurry by.

VIRGINIA REEL

In Clarke County, the story goes, the family name
Was saved by a single crop of wheat,
The houses and land kept in a clear receipt for the subsequent suicides,
The hard times and non-believers to qualify and disperse:
Woodburn and Cedar Hall, Smithfield, Auburn and North Hill:
Names like white moths kicked up from the tall grass,
Spreading across the countryside
From the Shenandoah to Charles Town and the Blue Ridge.

And so it happened. But none of us lives here now, in any of them,
Though Aunt Roberta is still in town,
Close to the place my great-great-grandfather taught Nelly Custis's
    children once
Answers to Luther. And Cardinal Newman too.
Who cares? Well, I do. It's worth my sighs
To walk here, on the wrong road, tracking a picture back
To its bricks and its point of view.
It's worth my while to be here, crumbling this dirt through my bare
    hands.

I've come back for the first time in twenty years,
Sand in my shoes, my pockets full of the same wind

That brought me before, my flesh
Remiss in the promises it made then, the absolutes it's heir to.
This is the road they drove on. And this is the rise
Their blood repaired to, removing its gloves.
And this is the dirt their lives were made of, the dirt the world is,
Immeasurable emptiness of all things.

I stand on the porch of Wickliffe Church,
My kinfolk out back in the bee-stitched vines and weeds,
The night coming on, my flat shirt drawing the light in,
Bright bud on the branch of nothing's tree.
In the new shadows, memory starts to shake out its dark cloth.
Everyone settles down, transparent and animate,
Under the oak trees.
Hampton passes the wine around, Jaq toasts to our health.

And when, from the blear and glittering air,
A hand touches my shoulder,
I want to fall to my knees, and keep on falling, here,
Laid down by the articles that bear my names,
The limestone and marble and locust wood.
But that's for another life. Just down the road, at Smithfield, the last of
    the apple blossoms
Fishtails to earth through the shot twilight,
A little vowel for the future, a signal from us to them.

GATE CITY BREAKDOWN

Like a vein of hard coal, it was the strike
We fantasized, the pocket of sure reward we sidestepped the
    roadblocks for
In Southwest Virginia, seamed in its hillside
Above the north fork of the Holston River.

One afternoon before Christmas
In 1953, we crossed the bridge from Tennessee on a whiskey run,

Churchill and Bevo Hammond and Philbeck and I,
All home for the holidays.
On the back road where they chased us, we left the Sheriff's Patrol in
   their own dust,
And washed ours down with Schlitz on the way home.

Jesus, it's so ridiculous, and full of self-love,
The way we remember ourselves,
                  and the dust we leave . . .

Remember me as you will, but remember me once
Slide-wheeling around the curves,
                letting it out on the other side of the line.

CLINCHFIELD STATION

The road unwinds like a bandage.
These are the benchmarks:
A letter from Yucatan, a ball,
The chairs of the underlife.

Descent is a fact of speech,
A question of need—lampblack, cold-drill,
A glint in the residue:
Dante explained it, how

It bottoms out, becoming a threshold,
The light like a damp confetti,
The wind an apostrophe, the birds
Stone bone in the smooth-limbed trees.
        *

Mums in a vase, flakes in a hope chest:
Father advise us, sift our sins—
Ferry us back and step down;
Dock at the Clinchfield Station:

Our Lady of Knoxville reclines there
On her hard bed; a golf club
Hums in the grass. The days, dry cat tracks, come round,
A silence beneath the leaves:

The way back is always into the earth.
Hornbeam or oak root, the ditch, the glass:
It all comes to the same thing:
A length of chain, a white hand.

CHRISTMAS EAST OF THE BLUE RIDGE

So autumn comes to an end with these few wet sad stains
Stuck to the landscape,
                                    December dark
Running its hands through the lank hair of late afternoon,
Little tongues of the rain holding forth
                                    under the eaves,
Such wash, such watery words . . .

So autumn comes to this end,
And winter's vocabulary, downsized and distanced,
Drop by drop
Captures the conversation with its monosyllabic gutturals
And tin music,
                    gravelly consonants, scratched vowels.

Soon the camel drivers will light up their fires, soon the stars
Will start on their brief dip down from the back of heaven,
Down to the desert's dispensation
And night reaches, the gall and first birth,
The second only one word from now,
                                    one word and its death from right now.

Meanwhile, in Charlottesville, the half-moon
Hums like a Hottentot
                    high over Monticello,
Clouds dishevel and rag out,
The alphabet of our discontent
Keeps on with its lettering,
                    gold on the black walls of our hearts . . .

Acknowledgments

A. R. Ammons' "I Went Back," from his *Worldly Hopes* (Copyright ©
1982 by A. R. Ammons); "This Black Rich Country" and "Mountain
Talk," from his *Collected Poems, 1951–1971* (Copyright © 1972 by
A. R. Ammons); and "Gravelly Run," from his *Selected Poems, Ex-
panded Edition* (Copyright © 1987, 1977, 1975, 1974, 1972, 1971,
1970, 1966, 1965, 1964, 1955 by A. R. Ammons) are used by permission
of W. W. Norton & Co., Inc. "Enfield Falls" first appeared in *Gettysburg
Review,* and "Alligator Holes Down Along About Old Dock" first ap-
peared in *North Carolina Literary Review;* these poems are reprinted by
permission of the respective journals and of Mrs. Phyllis Ammons.

All of James Applewhite's poems in this collection have been pub-
lished previously by Louisiana State University Press: "Road Down
Home" in *Ode to the Chinaberry Tree* (1986); "A Map of Simplicities"
and "*Southland* Drive-In" in *Foreseeing the Journey* (1983); and "A Wil-
son County Farmer," "The Village After Sunset," "Water from the Lamp
Bottle," and "Home Team" in *A History of the River* (1993). Reprinted
by permission of LSU Press and the author.

"The Sycamore," "Air and Fire," "History," "Stay Home," and "In Rain" are reprinted from *The Selected Poems of Wendell Berry* (Counterpoint, 1998) by permission of Perseus Books Group.

Fred Chappell's "Remembering Wind Mountain at Sunset," from *Midquest* (LSU Press, 1981), and "Abandoned Schoolhouse on Long Branch," from *Spring Garden* (LSU Press, 1995), are reprinted by permission of LSU Press and the author.

Kelly Cherry's "On Watching a Young Man Play Tennis" is reprinted from *Lovers and Agnostics* (Red Clay Books, 1975; Carnegie Mellon University Press, 1995) by permission of the author. "For Teen-Age Boys Murdered in Texas" is reprinted from *Relativity: A Point of View* (LSU Press, 1977; Carnegie Mellon University Press, 2000) by permission of the author. "How to Wait" and "The Rose," from *Natural Theology* (LSU Press, 1988), and "In the Garden by the Sea: Easter" and "Waiting for the End of Time," from *God's Loud Hand* (LSU Press, 1993), are reprinted by permission of LSU Press and the author.

James Dickey's poems "Hunting Civil War Relics at Nimblewill Creek," "Snow on a Southern State," "In the Marble Quarry," and "At Darien Bridge" are reprinted from *The Whole Motion: Collected Poems 1945–1992* (Wesleyan University Press, 1992) by permission of Wesleyan University Press.

"Old Slavemarket: St. Augustine, Fla.," "Rugby Road," and "For a Bitter Season" are reprinted from *The Collected Poems of George Garrett* (University of Arkansas Press, 1984) by permission of the author.

Andrew Hudgins' poems in this collection have been published previously in journals: "Flamingos Have Arrived in Ashtabula" in *Descant,* "Southern Literature" in *Southern Review,* "The Hawk above the House" in *Atlantic Monthly,* "The Chinaberry Trees" in *Southern Cultures,* and "The Young Oaks" in *Paris Review*. They are reprinted by permission of the author.

T. R. Hummer's "The Antichrist in Arkansas," "Plate Glass," and "Mechanics" are reprinted from *Walt Whitman in Hell* (LSU Press, 1996) by permission of LSU Press and the author.

"Carpe Diem," from *Transparent Gestures* by Rodney Jones, copyright © 1989 by Rodney Jones, and "Failed Memory Exercise," from

Apocalyptic Narrative by Rodney Jones, copyright © 1993 by Rodney Jones, are reprinted by permission of Houghton Mifflin Company. All rights reserved.

Yusef Komunyakaa's "Yellow Dog Café," "Looking for Choctaw," "Gristmill," and "Knights of the White Camellia & Deacons of Defense," from *Magic City* (Wesleyan University Press, 1992), and "Villon/ Leadbelly" and "Work," from *Neon Vernacular* (University Press of New England, 1993), are reprinted here by permission of the author. All of these poems have also appeared in *Pleasure Dome* (Wesleyan University Press, 2001).

Robert Morgan's "The Road from Elmira" and "Mica County," from *Sigodlin* (Wesleyan University Press, 1990), and "Jutaculla Rock," "Horace Kephart," and "Man and Machine," from *At the Edge of the Orchard Country* (Wesleyan University Press, 1987), are reprinted by permission of the author.

George Scarbrough's "Letter to Spencer," "Cutting Sod-Land," "Eastward in Estanalle," "The Storm," "Field Beyond the Ridge," and "Hymn for the Sound of Hymns" are reprinted from *Tellico Blue* (E. P. Dutton, 1949; reprint, Iris Press, 1999) by permission of the author.

Dave Smith's "New Orleans Engagement," "The Louisiana Sea of Faith," "Night Traffic near Winchester, Virginia," "Cumberland Station," and "On a Field Trip at Fredericksburg," are reprinted from *The Wick of Memory: New and Selected Poems, 1970–2000* (LSU Press, 2000) by permission of LSU Press and the author.

Henry Taylor's "At South Fork Cemetery," from *Understanding Fiction: Poems, 1986–1996* (LSU Press, 1996), and "A Bargain at Half the Price," "Goodbye to Old Friends," "The Hughesville Scythe," and "Buildings and Grounds," from *The Horse Show at Midnight and An Afternoon of Pocket Billiards* (LSU Press, 1992), are reprinted by permission of LSU Press and the author.

"Visiting the Graves," "Stone Pond," and "At the Movie: Virginia, 1956," are from *The Lotus Flowers* by Ellen Bryant Voigt. Copyright © 1987 by Ellen Bryant Voigt. Used by permission of W. W. Norton Company, Inc. "The Spring" and "Blue Ridge" are from *The Forces of Plenty* by Ellen Bryant Voigt. Copyright © 1983 by Ellen Bryant Voigt. Used by permission of W. W. Norton Company, Inc. "House" is reprinted from *Claiming Kin* (Wesleyan University Press, 1976) by permission of Wesleyan University Press and the author.

"Holly and Hickory," "The Well House," "In Moonlight, Somewhere, They Are Singing," "In Italian, They Call the Bird *Civetta*," "Sitting on Farm Lawn on Sunday Afternoon," and "Was It One of the Long Hunters of Kentucky Who Discovered Boone at Sunset," copyright © 1958, 1980, 1983 by Robert Penn Warren, are reprinted from *The Collected Poems of Robert Penn Warren* (LSU Press, 1998) by permission of William Morris Agency, Inc., on behalf of the author.

Charles Wright's "Hardin County," from *Bloodlines* (Wesleyan University Press, 1975); "Virginia Reel" and "Gate City Breakdown," from *The Southern Cross* (Random House, 1981); "Clinchfield Station," from *Hard Freight* (Wesleyan University Press, 1973); and "Christmas East of the Blue Ridge," from *Black Zodiac* (Noonday Press/Farrar, Straus, and Giroux, 1997), are reprinted by permission of the author.

Contributors

A. R. AMMONS wrote nearly thirty books of poetry. His *Collected Poems 1951–1971* received a National Book Award and the Library of Congress' Rebekah Johnson Bobbitt National Prize for Poetry. *Garbage* (1993) also won a National Book Award. *A Coast of Trees* (1981) received the National Book Critics Circle Award for Poetry, and for *Sphere* (1972) Ammons was awarded the Bollingen Prize. His many other honors included the Wallace Stevens Award, the Poetry Society of America's Robert Frost Medal, the Ruth Lilly Prize, and fellowships from the Guggenheim Foundation, the MacArthur Foundation, and the American Academy of Arts and Letters. He was Goldwin Smith Professor of Poetry at Cornell University until his retirement in 1998. A. R. Ammons died on February 25, 2002.

JAMES APPLEWHITE has received the Associated Writing Programs Contemporary Poetry Prize, the American Academy and Institute of Arts and Letters Jean Stein Award in Poetry, the Roanoke-Chowan Poetry Award, the Governor's North Carolina Award in Literature, and a Guggenheim fellowship. He is the author of nine books of poetry, including *Lessons in Soaring* (1989), *Daytime and Starlight* (1997), and *Quartet for Three Voices* (2002). He is a professor of English at Duke University.

WENDELL BERRY is a conservationist and the author of numerous books, including novels as well as collections of poetry and essays. His poetry collections include his *Collected Poems, 1957–1982* (1985), *Traveling at Home* (1989), *Entries* (1984), and *A Timbered Choir: The Sabbath Poems, 1979–1997*. He has taught at New York University and at the University of Kentucky. Among his honors and awards are fellowships from the Guggenheim and Rockefeller Foundations, the National Institute and Academy of Arts and Letters Award, the T. S. Eliot Award, a Lannan Foundation Award, and a grant from the National Endowment for the Arts.

FRED CHAPPELL, poet and novelist, is a native of western North Carolina and teaches at the University of North Carolina at Greensboro. His books of poetry include *The World between the Eyes* (1971), *Wind Mountain* (1979), *Midquest* (1981), *Spring Garden: New and Selected Poems* (1995), and *Family Gathering* (2000). He has received the Bollingen Prize, the Aiken Taylor Prize, and many other awards for his writing.

KELLY CHERRY, a winner of the Fellowship's Hanes Prize for Poetry, is the author of several books of poetry, including *God's Loud Hand* (1993), *Death and Transfiguration* (1997), and *Rising Venus* (2002); novels, including *Augusta Played* (1979) and *My Life and Dr. Joyce Brothers* (1990); a book of essays, *Writing the World* (1995); and an autobiography, *The Exiled Heart* (1991). She lives in Virginia.

JAMES DICKEY wrote over a dozen volumes of poetry, including *Buckdancer's Choice*, which won the National Book Award and the Poetry Society of America's Melville Cane Award. He served as Poetry Consultant to the Library of Congress from 1966 to 1968 and was a fellow of the American Academy of Arts and Letters and of the National Institute of Arts and Letters. He received the Harriet Monroe Poetry Award in 1996. James Dickey died in 1996 after a long illness.

GEORGE GARRETT is a prolific author and editor whose many works include novels and short story collections, collections of essays, stage plays, and screenplays. Much of his poetry can be found in *The Collected Poems of George Garrett* (1984) and *Days of Our Lives Lie in Fragments: New and Old Poems, 1957–1997*. His fiction includes the novels *The Finished Man* (1959), *Do, Lord, Remember Me* (1965), and *The King of Babylon Shall Not Come Against You* (1996); *An Evening Performance: New and Selected Stories* (1985); and *The Magic Striptease* (1973), three novellas. Having served as Henry Hoyns Professor of Creative Writing at the University of Virginia, he is now retired from teaching and lives in Charlottesville.

ANDREW HUDGINS has received the Witter Bynner Award for Poetry, the Fellowship's Hanes Prize for Poetry, and fellowships from the Bread Loaf Writers' Conference, the Ingram Merrill Foundation, and the National Endowment for the Arts. His poetry collections include *Saints and Strangers* (1985), *The Never-Ending: New Poems* (1991), *The Glass Hammer: A Southern Childhood* (1994), and *Babylon in a Jar* (1998). He teaches at Ohio State University.

T. R. HUMMER has published seven collections of poetry, including *Walt Whitman in Hell* (1996), which won the Fellowship's Hanes Prize for Poetry, and his most recent, *Useless Virtues* (2001). His poetry has appeared in the *Paris Review, New Yorker, Parnassus,* and *Ploughshares,* among other publications. A recipient of fellowships from the Guggenheim Foundation and the National Endowment for the Arts as well as two Pushcart Prizes, Hummer is editor-in-chief of the *Georgia Review.*

RODNEY JONES is the author of seven books of poetry, including *Transparent Gestures* (1989), which won National Book Critics Circle Award; *Apocalyptic Narrative and Other Poems* (1993); *Elegy for the Southern Drawl* (1999); and *Kingdom of the Instant* (2002). He has received a Guggenheim fellowship, the Lavan Award of the American Academy of Arts and Letters, and the Jean Stein Award of the American Academy and Institute of Arts and Letters. He is a professor of creative writing at Southern Illinois University in Carbondale.

YUSEF KOMUNYAKAA received the Fellowship's Hanes Prize for Poetry in 1997. numerous books of poems include *Neon Vernacular: New and Selected Poems 1977–1989* (1994), for which he received the Pulitzer Prize and the Kingsley Tufts Poetry Award; *Pleasure Dome: New and Collected Poems, 1975–1999; Thieves of Paradise* (1998), which was a finalist for the National Book Critics Circle Award; and *Talking Dirty to the Gods* (2000). Other honors include the William Faulkner Prize from the Université de Rennes, the Thomas Forcade Award, and fellowships from the Fine Arts Work Center in Provincetown, the Louisiana Arts Council, and the National Endowment for the Arts. He is a professor in the creative writing program at Princeton University.

ROBERT MORGAN, Kappa Alpha Professor of English at Cornell University, is the author of numerous works of poetry and fiction, including the novel *Gap Creek* (1999) and short story collection *The Balm of Gilead Tree* (1999). His poetry collections include *Sigodlin* (1990), and *Green River: New and Selected Poems* (1991), and *Topsoil Road* (2000); his poems have also appeared in *Poetry, Paris Review, Atlantic Monthly, American Poetry Review,* and elsewhere. He has received the Fellowship's Hanes Prize for Poetry, the North Carolina Award in Literature, and Guggenheim, Rockefeller, and National Endowment for the Arts fellowships for his work.

GEORGE SCARBROUGH is the winner of the Fellowship's James Still Award for 2001. His poems have appeared in more than sixty-five magazines and journals. He has published five books of poetry, including *Tellico Blue* (1949), *Summer So-Called* (1956), and *Invitation to Kim* (1989), which was nominated for a Pulitzer Prize. He is also author of the novel *A Summer Ago* (1986).

DAVE SMITH is the author of numerous collections of poetry and criticism and the novel *Onliness*. His poetry collections include *Fate's Kite: Poems, 1991–1995; Floating on Solitude* (1996); *The Wick of Memory: New and Selected Poems 1970–2000*. He has been awarded fellowships from the National Endowment for the Arts, the Guggenheim Foundation, the Rockefeller Foundation, and the Lyndhurst Foundation.

HENRY TAYLOR is professor of literature and codirector of the M.F.A. program in creative writing at American University in Washington, D.C. His third collection of poetry, *The Flying Change* (1985), received the Pulitzer Prize. His other poetry collections include *The Horse Show at Midnight* (1966), *An Afternoon of Pocket Billiards* (1975), and *Understanding Fiction: Poems, 1986–1996*.

ELLEN BRYANT VOIGT is the author of six collections of poetry, most recently *Shadows of Heaven*, as well as a collection of essays on craft. She has received the Fellowship's Hanes Prize for Poetry as well as an Academy of American Poets fellowship, grants from the Vermont Council on the Arts, the National Endowment for the Arts, and the Guggenheim Foundation, and a Pushcart Prize. Since 1981 she has taught in the M.F.A. program for writers at Warren Wilson College, and she is the Vermont State Poet.

ROBERT PENN WARREN, poet, novelist, and critic, is the only writer to have won the Pulitzer Prize in both fiction (for *All the King's Men* in 1947) and poetry (for *Promises: Poems 1954–1956* in1958 and for *Now and Then: Poems 1976–1978* in 1979). During his teaching tenure at Louisiana State University, 1934–1942, he cofounded the *Southern Review*, and in 1985 he was named America's first Poet Laureate. After a long and prolific career, Robert Penn Warren died in 1989.

CHARLES WRIGHT has published more than ten collections of poetry. His *Selected Early Poems* (1983) won the National Book Award. His other books of poetry include *Chickamauga* (1996), which won the Lenore Marshall Poetry Prize; *Black Zodiac* (1997), which won the Pulitzer

Prize and the Los Angeles *Times* Book Prize; and his most recent, *Negative Blue* (2000). He has also been awarded the American Academy of Arts and Letters Award of Merit Medal and the Ruth Lilly Poetry Prize. In 1999 he was elected a chancellor of The Academy of American Poets. He is Souder Family Professor of English at the University of Virginia in Charlottesville.